Going Intergenerational

All Ages Learning Bible Truths Together

by Jim Teeters

- Guidelines for success
  - Helpful ideas and resources
    - Twenty take-and-teach programs

Going Intergenerational

All Ages Learning Bible Truths Together

© 2010 by Jim Teeters

BARCLAY PRESS
Newberg, OR

www.barclaypress.com

All rights reserved. No part may be reproduced for any commercial purpose by any method without permission in writing from the copyright holder.

All Scripture quotations, unless otherwise indicated, are taken from the *Holy Bible, New International Version*®. *NIV*®. Copyright © 1973, 1978, 1984 by Biblica, Inc.™ Used by permission of Zondervan. All rights reserved worldwide. www.zondervan.com.

Scripture quotations marked (CEV) are from the *Contemporary English Version* © 1991, 1992, 1995 by American Bible Society. Used with Permission

Scripture quotations from *THE MESSAGE*. Copyright © by Eugene H. Peterson 1993, 1994, 1995, 1996, 2000, 2001, 2002. Used by permission of NavPress Publishing Group.

ISBN 978-1-59498-021-3

ACKNOWLEDGMENTS

I offer special thanks to Ann O'Neal Garcia for her encouragement and skilled writer's edits. I thank Laurie Conant for her encouragement and persistence in seeing the value of this work. I am indebted to the hundreds of enthusiastic participants in intergenerational programs I have led—they are the "proof of the pudding" in showing the value of these experiences. Thanks, also to Pastor Paul Meier who invited me year after year to direct the family camp programs at Quaker Cove Friends Conference Grounds in northwest Washington. Thanks to Barclay Press under the direction of Dan McCracken for making this book a reality. And finally, I enjoy the support of my wife Rebecca, who has often lent her musical talents to intergenerational programs throughout the years.

TABLE OF CONTENTS

Prologue | iv

Introduction | **1**

Chapter One   All Ages Learning Together: An Example | **2**

Chapter Two   Benefits of Intergenerational Programming | **8**

Chapter Three   Principles of Intergenerational Programming | **12**

Chapter Four   Teach the Way Jesus Taught | **19**

Chapter Five   Twelve Interactive Learning Methods for All Ages | **27**

Chapter Six   Lesson-Planning Process | **33**

Chapter Seven   Design and Develop | **39**

RESOURCES

Resource 1   Twenty Sample Intergenerational Programs | **49**

Resource 2   Fourteen Scripture Outlines for Intergenerational Programs | **71**

Resource 3   Poetry as Prayer Intergenerational Program | **74**

Resource 4   Intergenerational Programming in a Family Camp | **79**

Resource 5   'Alice the Camel' Game | **85**

Resource 6   Elevator to Judgment Drama | **86**

Resource 7   Parable of the Sower (Combined Scripture) | **88**

Resource 8   Poem: The Sword of the Spirit | **89**

Resource 9   Warm-up Activities for All Ages | **90**

PROLOGUE

Illustrations and Examples

The illustrations and examples of programs I have either taken from real situations as well as I remember them, or I have created situations to show how to use this method. My aim is to teach, so the illustrations and examples—real or imagined—are provided as tools for your learning.

Be Creative

The illustrations, examples, and sample programs are only suggested ways to proceed. Leaders and/or planning committees should use their own creative abilities and local situation to modify or expand on the suggestions. You may have electronic projectors or other resources you can use—substitute those when I mention flipcharts. Let your creative juices start to flow—break out of the mold, think outside the box!

Two Ways to Plan

Intergenerational programming can be done in two ways. The leader can design, facilitate, and teach each program. The second way is that the participants can do much of the planning and teaching with the leader acting as encourager and facilitator. Either way is fine, but the latter approach is more powerful in identifying and developing leaders.

INTRODUCTION

Go Intergenerational

*Adults offer wisdom, children offer joy.
Now that's a winning combination!*

This book challenges conventional wisdom that separates learners by age and offers a new way to teach and inspire kids, youth, and adults! The usual way of Christian education is based on the belief that age groups should not be mixed—kids are kids and adults are adults and never the twain shall meet. The disciples certainly believed that when they thought it was prudent to keep children out of the way of the "adult business" of the Savior. But Jesus had another idea:

People were bringing little children to Jesus to have him touch them, but the disciples rebuked them. When Jesus saw this, he was indignant. He said to them, "Let the little children come to me, and do not hinder them, for the kingdom of God belongs to such as these. I tell you the truth; anyone who will not receive the kingdom of God like a little child will never enter it." And he took the children in his arms, put his hands on them and blessed them. (Mark 10:13-16)

I guess it is important to Jesus that we mingle with little children! Further, we must become *like them* to enter the kingdom of God, so it would be best for adults and children to be together in order for adults to bless the little children and learn from them!

In my opinion the generation gap we hear about happens because adults and kids stay separated. When adults and kids play and learn together, bridges are built and the gap disappears. So you might ask, "What should we do?" The book you are holding addresses that question. Just start turning pages and learn how you and your church or community can use Intergenerational Programming to find wisdom and joy.

CHAPTER ONE

All Ages Learning Together: An Example

Treasures in Heaven

"Welcome, everyone, to our program," Frank, the leader, greets the group.

The "group" is a gathering of three preschoolers, five elementary school kids, a couple of young teens, one high school senior, and five adults including one ninety-year-old man seated in a wheelchair. Counting the leader, that makes a gathering of seventeen folks in all. They are meeting in the large classroom near the back of the church; it is the Christian education hour at Milltown Friends Church, and Frank leads the group this month.

On the flipchart at the front of the classroom is today's Scripture:

"Do not store up for yourselves treasures on earth, where moth and rust destroy, and where thieves break in and steal. But store up for yourselves treasures in heaven, where moth and rust do not destroy, and where thieves do not break in and steal. *For where your treasure is there your heart will be also.*" (Matt. 6:19-21, emphasis added)

In the front of the room there is also a large cardboard box, decorated to look like a treasure chest in a pirate movie. The younger kids are looking at it very closely and chatting. Frank stands before the group and starts the lesson.

"What do you suppose is in this treasure chest?" he asks, glancing around the room, ready for anyone of any age to answer. All the young kids raise their hands and wave them wildly. He points at Lucy.

"Lucy, what's in here?"

"It's gold!"

"No, it's jewels," says Kenny, the sixth grader.

"I am guessing some delicious snack," offers Malinda, Lucy's mom.

"Nothing," says Carlos, a young teen.

Frank takes more guesses and then says, "Well, we are going to find out at the end of our class. But first let me have a couple of volunteers read our Scripture." Barb raises her hand, as does Mr. Coupo, the ninety-year-old. Barb reads the first sentence, Mr. Coupo the second, then both read together the last sentence. Frank asks everyone who can read, to read together the last sentence loudly and clearly; then he asks them to read it two additional times, more loudly!

Then Frank draws a big heart on the next sheet of flipchart paper, rips it off, and stuffs it stealthily into the treasure chest. The kids strain to see inside.

"Oh, no, you don't!" says Frank, "We'll see in there soon enough, and just maybe, we can all take some treasure home with us." With that, Frank opens the next section of the lesson.

Frank asks the class to break into four small groups and assigns an adult and a youth in each group with a couple of the young kids. Then he asks each group to make a list of treasures they have that could break, get rusty, or get stolen. He hands out marking pens and a big flipchart sheet to each group, and he asks the teens to take notes. After a few minutes, Frank asks the groups to list the kinds of treasures that would never break, spoil, rust, or get stolen. This is a little more difficult and there are some puzzled looks.

Frank adds this incentive: "Whichever group can come up with the most 'treasures in heaven,' will get first look into the treasure chest." This sets the groups to more diligent discussion, and even the pre-schoolers seem eager to offer ideas.

After a few minutes, Frank asks the groups to post the lists of "treasures on earth" at the front of the room. There are plenty of ideas: cars, toys, clothes, iPods, Nintendo Wiis, and all kinds of things folks like to collect. Frank asks if any of these items can be found in heaven. There is a resounding, "No!"

"Okay," Frank challenges, "let's see who gets to look first in the treasure chest. What ideas do you have for treasures in heaven?"

The lists include: love, joy, peace, forgiveness, happiness, Holy Spirit, God's love, salvation, and helping others. Mr. Coupo's group has the longest list, so the box is brought over to Mr. Coupo to open but he defers to Matthew, a preschooler. The tension builds as Matthew stands before the box and waits.

"Go ahead and open it, Matthew," says Frank.

"Cupcakes!" yells Matthew.

Each richly decorated cupcake includes a little card with the last sentence of the Scripture. Everyone is quite excited.

Frank watches as each person gingerly peels back the paper wrappers and nibbles on the cupcakes. The adults and youth help the younger ones. When the cupcakes are eaten, Frank stands before the group.

"Could you give me the cupcakes back?" he asks. Everyone looks puzzled. "Well, of course not," says Frank. "That treasure is not one you can take to heaven—when it's gone, it's gone!"

He continues, "But what about the items we've listed here?" He points to the "heaven" lists. "Now where do you want your heart to be? With the cupcakes or with these: love, joy, peace...?"

He points to Lucy for a response.

"Well, not with the cupcakes, 'cause they're gone," she smiles.

Frank asks the group to applaud. "Out of the mouth of babes!" he says.

"So," Frank continues, "let's remember this week to pay attention to those things we can have in our hearts, and those things we may need or want but that will never be a part of heaven. The greatest treasure is Jesus in our hearts and the love he gives us."

Frank asks Misty to lead the group in a song: "Oh, How He Loves You and Me" and "Jesus Loves Me."

Frank asks if anyone would like to pray, and Jake raises his hand and prays:

"Jesus, we thank you for cupcakes, but mostly for your love that we can take all the way to your heaven. Remind us this week that where our treasure is, so is our heart. Also, thanks for Lucy's lesson."

Deconstructing "Treasures in Heaven"

The lesson above is designed using Larry Richards's model of Christian education.* It is a simple and useful model for designing lessons for intergenerational groups, which I highly recommend. Here is a brief description:

HOOK – Get learners interested in the topic.

BOOK – Refer to, read, or tell about a passage in the Bible.

LOOK – Use a discussion, activity, or questions to draw out the meaning of the Scripture.

TOOK – Grasp the application of the lesson to take and use in daily life.

Let's break down the "Treasures in Heaven" lesson:

- HOOK – When Frank prepared the "treasure chest" and asked participants to guess what was in the box, he was applying the "hook" approach. He was getting the group interested in the lesson to come. This approach was designed to reach all ages; the kids and adults were interested in what was in the box.

- BOOK – When Frank prepared the Scripture passage on a flipchart and had the participants read the Scripture, he was using the "book" approach. He was making sure the Scripture was presented.

- LOOK – When Frank asked the participants to get into small groups and list the various treasures, offering incentive for them to come up with a long list, he used the "look" approach. He was using an active learning method to engage the participants with the Bible truth.

- TOOK – When Frank summed up the learning and asked the question "Where do you want your heart to be?" he was beginning the "took" approach and encouraging the participants of all ages to consider using this scriptural truth in everyday life.

The beauty of this HOOK, BOOK, LOOK, TOOK model is its simplicity: It is easy to remember and apply. Combining this approach with the methods presented in this book provides a very usable way to design Intergenerational Programs.

---

*Lawrence O. Richards and Gary J. Bredfelt, *Creative Bible Teaching* (revised and expanded), Chicago, IL: Moody Bible Institute, 1998, Chapter Nine.

All Ages Learn at Different Levels but Can Learn Together

Let's use as an example the story of Solomon who, when confronted by two women claiming to be the mother of an infant, ordered the child to be cut in half and shared between the two mothers. The true mother then protested and offered her child to the false mother. This woman's great concern for the child's life revealed to the court that she was, indeed, the true mother. Here is a sampling of the kinds of lessons various age groupings can learn (Figure 1.1).

You can see that people of any age can learn valuable lessons from the same Scripture passage. The leader can ask various questions or can direct activities that produce learning from each age group. In Chapter Three we will explore establishing the AIM for each lesson.

figure 1.1

AGES	LESSON LEARNED	GUIDELINES
Early childhood	It is best to tell the truth.	Teach simple lessons to point out right from wrong.
Late childhood	Truth-telling is rewarded; lying results in defeat or humiliation.	Help children understand the consequences of choices they make.
Youth	Explore feelings of both mothers. Discuss making better choices in our lives.	Facilitate exploration and decision making based on Scripture. Show how Scripture applies to life issues.
Adults	What is wisdom? How can we become wiser? Make wise decisions.	Explore the deeper meaning of Scripture and how to apply transformative truth to everyday life.

An Invitation to Use
Intergenerational Programming in Your Church

In Chapter Two, I will introduce you to the benefits of Intergenerational Programming and invite you to use this in your church. Besides being a marvelous way to learn generally, Intergenerational Programming (IP) provides a way for small churches to have a Christian education (CE) hour with only a small group of people. You can use this method with kids of all ages together, and therefore expand your CE program. Some small churches have perhaps one or two kids in any age category and need to recruit several teachers to cover these classes. But with IP you can use fewer teachers and get much-needed CE lessons taught.

You may ask: What if our youth need to spend time by themselves? This may be very important for youth or adults. The IP can be modified to occur at intervals (two Sundays per month) or you can have a portion of your program be IP and for the other portion participants return to same-age groupings. I encourage you to use your imagination. There is no "one-size-fits-all" approach. Be flexible and spend time examining and planning for the unique needs of your congregation.

If IP is offered as one of the options in your CE program, then adults can choose to participate in it. This could be a wonderful way to introduce parents to CE and to see what their children are learning. Your congregation could also use IP as a way of integrating new folks into your church program.

The marvelous thing about Scripture is that there are no age barriers when it comes to God's truth. Everyone can learn and there is no reason why all ages can't learn these truths together. I invite you to try it out!

CHAPTER TWO

Benefits of Intergenerational Programming

Christian education (CE) has traditionally emphasized separating the ages. The idea seems to be that kids do "kid stuff" and adults do "adult stuff" and the two shouldn't mix. Since it is adults doing the planning, adults seem to have the idea that involving kids might mean less meaningful learning. The kids might be invited to hear a story during worship services before they are dismissed, and then adults do their thing and kids do theirs. But have you noticed how attracted adults are to the kids' story as well? Most often they listen with as much interest as the kids. Everybody likes stories—we learn that way. Jesus was well aware of that because this is how he taught adults—with stories and illustrations as well as with other methods we'll explore in Chapter Four.

It is true that math, reading, or writing must be learned in stages and so our public education is thus divided into beginning and advanced classes that, by nature, usually follow the age span. But learning life's truth is open to any age, and both adults and children can learn from each other. The point is, separating ages is not a proven way to learn scriptural truth. It is just a tradition invented by adults, not a definitive fact. Let's challenge that habit by looking at the benefits of Intergenerational Programming (IP).

Participant Involvement

Most of my experience with IP has been in family camps where traditionally adults listen to talks given by leaders and the kids are trundled off to their own classes or special activities. But one time, many years ago, I was invited to attend a family camp with all ages learning together. It was an eye-opener for me. The sessions were outlined by the camp planners, but the actual lessons (they were called "events") were planned by the campers—both kids and adults. Teaching kids demands involvement and active learning, and the adults jumped right in. Everyone had fun and learned, too. This is true with an Intergenerational

Programming session. It demands that people get involved just as we saw in the lesson "Treasures in Heaven" at the beginning of this book. People learn best when they are engaged, involved, and active in the process. When participants take part in planning the lessons, the learning is multiplied. The greater the involvement by participants, the greater the learning. That is a maxim proven over and over in education. When learning involves the whole person, greater learning and more change is possible. You can involve participants of any age, but when kids are a part of the mix, active learning is necessary.

Everyone Has Fun

Mixing the age groups automatically results in fun. Kids and youth like to have fun and laugh, so it's no surprise that adults find they are having fun and laughing too. Happiness and enthusiasm provide a good atmosphere for learning. Often we separate the kids partly to relieve parents from the constant burden of child caring. What I have found is that when you add a mix of adults and kids, the job of discipline and child caring becomes easier. Everyone gets in the act and the parents are relieved of the some of their burden. Sometimes families can stay in the same group together and at other times kids can have other adults to relate to.

There Are a Variety of Ways to Use IP in Your Church

The CE hour is only one place to use IP. Wherever kids, youth, and adults gather, fun and meaningful Bible learning can take place! Here are some other ways to use it:

Family camps – Create memorable events.

Vacation Bible school (VBS) – Involve all ages in VBS.

Family nights – Create a special event once per month.

Church picnics or outings – Make any event more exciting by adding special learning.

Worship service – Use a portion of the service to involve all ages or dedicate one worship service each calendar quarter to IP.

CE hour opening – Start each CE hour with a fun opening and add learning too.

Memorable Experiences

Think about it: How many lectures or sermons do you remember? You might remember a theme or perhaps a point or two. However, when kids and adults are engaged in fun, humorous, and exciting events, memories are built. "Oh, we wouldn't miss family camp," is something I have heard time and time again. People like to have fun and learn with groups of all ages. I can still remember events that took place long ago—when we were "swallowed by a whale" or saw the "walls come tumbling down." These events create permanent memories and remind us of the lessons we learned: *Obey God right away* and *with God great obstacles can be overcome!*

Build Relationships

One of the greatest benefits is how people connect. A youth may engage with a small kid in putting on a play, or an older adult may have an earnest discussion with a teenager. People get connected and build friendships. People doing things together creates bonds. Sitting in a classroom is not as bond-building as working together to construct a structure in a tower-building contest. Adults making up a song or poem with a couple of youth and a preschooler can create friendships—that "Hi, so glad to see you again Jody; some song we sang last Sunday, huh?" kind of connection.

The IP sessions are also great for helping church visitors get acquainted. Barriers get broken down quickly without the awkwardness so often found in those before- and after-the-service encounters. It is easy for people to say hello when they have to make a collage together.

Singles Fit Right In

Often in family camps (the title in our publicity is always "Friends and Family Camp") a person who is single can join a family or a family of unrelated people can be organized. Single people can quickly feel like they fit right in, and keeping the focus on activity and learning will help keep singles feeling comfortable.

Bible Truth Comes Alive

Bible truth comes alive when you can see it, hear it, feel it, even taste it! Often food plays a role in learning—not unlike the elements in the Passover meal. Fish and bread go along with the "loaves and fishes" miracle, salty snacks go along with being "salt and light." Participants build a tower for teaching on the Tower of Babel, and a leader distributes mustard seeds when he or she teaches about faith. The idea is to make lessons vivid, as we saw in the Introduction and with the treasure chest in the lesson on "Treasures in Heaven."

The Size of the Group Can Vary

One of the beauties of IP is that you can start small. Many small churches have few kids in each age during the CE hour. Often no CE hour is offered, or the CE hour is during the church service. With IP you can expand the group for teaching Bible lessons and as few as six to ten folks can make it work. The same powerful lessons, the same involvement, the same invitation to relationships or welcoming newcomers—it can happen with just a few people. In fact, this kind of program may very well be a way to build church attendance and improve the outreach efforts—"Come and have some fun at our church!"

Summary and Invitation to Try It

The "It's the way we've always done it!" attitude can create opposition in moving to more intergenerational activities. Recently I attended a church service where the congregation was seated around tables instead of in rows or in pews. This was a way to help people feel welcome and comfortable, and it provided a way to say to visitors, "This isn't like the churches you've rejected." Making the change took vision, imagination, and a willingness to think outside the box, and it was working because the congregation was growing and excited. Take a moment; read again the benefits of Intergenerational Programming and see if this might just be the next move for your church or religious education program.

CHAPTER THREE

Principles of Intergenerational Programming

When getting started with Intergenerational Programming (IP) there is a tendency to slip back into the "way we've always done it" mode because doing something new takes effort. The effort doesn't so much involve energy and work as it does changing one's point of view. Move slowly and experimentally as you integrate IP into your church educational program. The following principles will create better programming and greater success.

Teach to All Ages

To teach to all ages calls for paying attention to terms and illustrations, and avoiding some of the more disturbing aspects of Scripture (graphic depictions of violence or sexual references). First, you want to avoid using theological words without also including simpler explanations or descriptions. The term *salvation* could be phrased "all our bad behavior and thoughts are forgiven by God" or "Jesus introduces us to God as perfect." Or when Paul says God exalted Jesus, you might need to explain: "It's as if God pinned a big badge on Jesus that said: 'You are the best of the best!'" It is best to say the complex, yet add an explanation to reach the youngest ears. In doing so, you will reach those in the middle as well.

Illustrations also need to fit all ages. Once I taught a group of young girls and their camp counselors. I told them I would show them who God loves. I had them close their eyes and one by one I tapped each of them on the shoulder, and when they opened their eyes, I held a mirror in front of them. Some squealed with delight, and others got big smiles. Using drawings and pictures are helpful too. One time, when teaching how important each member of the body of Christ is, I drew a big ear on a flipchart and used it to illustrate to all age groups how silly it would be if the ear wanted to become the whole body.

There are some fairly graphic depictions of violence and sex in the Bible. Adults can handle these quite well, but with kids it is useful to avoid those passages or work around them in the story. The story of the rape of Tamar by Amnon, for instance, and stories of genocide are difficult to gloss over or explain. So when teaching children it is best to avoid these altogether. There are so many other exciting, touching, and inspiring stories in the Bible.

All Ages All the Time

Because there is a tendency to separate kids and adults, I reiterate the need to plan intentionally to have kids and adults together during the entire teaching time. Small groups should be organized so kids are included. The smallest ones (even infants) can be secure in arms or in strollers. The toddlers need to stay with a parent or another comforting, familiar person. But kids preschool age and older can fit right in. Just as if you were at a family gathering, these little ones are naturally present. The difference is that in a teaching situation, the little ones become an active part of the lesson along with adults.

Turn Students into Teachers

Place much of the action with the participants. A small group may write and perform a song or a skit to illustrate a lesson point. If you are teaching on the fruit of the Spirit, for example, each group can act out one of the fruits, such as love, joy, or peace. This way the participants teach each other. Confucius is famous for sahying: "What I hear, I forget, what I see, I remember, what I do, I understand." A well-known teacher added: "When I teach someone, I master what I have learned." That is a powerful idea, and educational research confirms there is a retention rate of about 90 percent when someone teaches the topic! So the more the participants teach, the greater the learning of that important Bible truth!

Directed or Discovery Teaching?

As a leader, you must be willing to not be the main show. There is a saying: "Don't be a sage on the stage, instead be the guide on the side." This is a tough role to play because it means you, as the teacher, must share the control for learning with the participants. You don't teach the truth—you help the participants *discover* the truth they will find in the rich learning grounds of Scripture. In the "Two Ways to Teach" chart (Figure 3.1), you can see how the role of the teacher in discovery learning differs from that in directed learning. There are times for both, but in IP the primary way is discovery.

figure 3.1

Two Ways to Teach

	Directed Learning	Discovery Learning
Goal	The goal is to lead students toward a predetermined end.	The goal is to open students to discovery.
Content	The content is the *focus* of all learning.	The content is the *catalyst* for discovery.
Teacher Role	The role of the teacher is to inform.	The role of the teacher is to create conditions for discovery.
Key Value	They key value is to find the right answer.	The key value is to help students find relevant answers.
Relationship	The teacher is to teach and the students are to learn.	The teacher joins with students in teaching and learning.
Conformity-Diversity	The teacher seeks conformity.	The teacher embraces diversity.
Control	Learning is dependent on control by the teacher.	Learning is dependent on shared control.
Culmination	The final stage is passing a test, completing an assignment, or graduating.	There is no final stage. Learning is a process that is continuously celebrated.

Create Interaction

Another key principle in Intergenerational Programming (IP) is to facilitate interaction among participants. You want kids and adults talking and doing things together. This is community building at the grass roots. Also, everyone is equal, as all are there to learn truths that can apply to life. So in that sense an elder, a pastor, and a three-year-old are interacting and learning together. In fact, each one learns something from the other, relationships are developed, stories are exchanged, and memories are made. The more people play and work together, the better. Consider ways to get people to relate to a wider group of people. Activities that encourage mixing up groups is good, so folks are encouraged to interact beyond their comfort zone. Using games, challenging assignments, and getting-acquainted activities will help here.

Laughing and Learning

Author Anne Lamott said laughter is carbonated holiness. And Charles Schultz made the tongue-in-cheek comment, "Try not to have fun…this is supposed to be educational." More and more educators are realizing that learning can and should be fun. We don't want anyone to be bored or to have a bad time in IP. This is a time for laughter and for fun. Once at a Christian family camp the biggest, meanest-looking ex-biker (who

---

figure 3.2

Laughing and Learning: How Humor Aids Learning

- Humor helps people relax.
- Humor puts people in a mood conducive to learning.
- Humor opens the mind.
- Humor awakens—it opens the air passages and blood vessels.
- Humor builds rapport; if you laugh with someone, barriers go down.
- Humor invites participation by raising the positive energy level.
- Humor warms us up and keeps us alert.
- Humor dissipates fears; it disarms our defenses.
- Humor is known to aid healing and wholeness.
- Humor makes difficult tasks easier—"a spoonful of sugar helps the medicine go down."
- Humor makes a point stick in the mind; laugh and it lasts.

was as sweet as pie) put cotton balls all over himself and came on hands and knees following the "Shepherd David" who was calling, "Here little sheepy, sheepy." This broke everyone into laughter, as you might imagine. But we learned about David as a shepherd and king during that lesson, and the picture has remained in my mind for more than twenty years!

Look at the list of ways humor aids learning in laughing and learning (Figure 3.2). Games, skits, contests, or singing create a powerful learning environment, and fun activities engage adults and kids alike.

Help the Adult "Become as a Child"

In IP there is an opportunity to help adults play, laugh, and learn in ways that help them develop humility and wonder. We enter the kingdom that way, according to Jesus. Adults can learn once more to see God as the comforting, loving parent—we are all his children. Jesus said "I tell you the truth, unless you change and become like little children, you will never enter the kingdom of heaven" (Matt. 18:3). What better way to prepare us for this than to be with and relate to children! In one family camp, groups of kids and adults played a game of "hide as a group." We scattered here and there trying to find places to hide—adults and kids together squeezing under bushes and behind buildings (the lesson was about David hiding from Saul, as I recall). What a scene, as kids and adults squealed and laughed together while trying not to be found by the "Sauls."

Help Children Learn from Adults

Kids see adults in authority roles mostly. In Intergenerational Programming kids can relate to adults as fellow learners, and adults lose some of the stigma of those big people who order them around. Adults become those who help, cooperate, and teach in fun and interesting ways. IP offers a more natural way for adults to engage with kids—not only as fellow learners but as gentle guides and helpers. When kids see adults in that light, they become more open and less resistant to learning from them.

Learning One Concept at a Time

The Intergenerational Programming lessons need to be clear, logical, and broken down into manageable units. Take the story of Jonah, which has many parts. Each part has something valuable to teach. The story of Jonah starts with a prophet getting a message from God to go to Nineveh and "preach against it" (Jonah 1:2). And Jonah runs away, not wanting to do as God directs. Well, that's enough for "part one" in a lesson. Adults alone might tackle the whole book in one lesson, but with kids in the IP setting, the more simple and clear the message, the better. We can all learn from Jonah, because there is some of Jonah in all of us (fear, anger, disappointment in life situations). We have many directives in Scripture, and we are also confronted with the "Word of the Lord" in our hearts, yet we ignore and these go our own way. The next lesson comes as we face the consequences of our disobedience to God. So IP works best with step-by-step sequencing, and careful planning of each lesson, one concept at a time. The power of each lesson is in the activities we plan that foster discoveries about God's truth in our lives.

Make Learning Active

Using active learning methods is a key in IP and we will spend more time on this particular principle in Chapter Five. Active learning methods means kids and adults are doing things, solving problems, putting truths into action, and having fun in the process.

I remember once being blindfolded and thrust inside a large fish (about sixty feet long, made of PVC pipe and black plastic sheeting). Each group of participants was pummeled with wet pillows, and then when we were all in the belly of the fish (or whale), we listened to Jonah pray. When we heard Jonah say, "What I have vowed I will make good" (Jonah 2:9) we all got ordered out—the large fish was regurgitating. That was "action!" After that we needed to tell about our experience and what it meant to us—what will we do to be more attuned to God's voice and to care about those who need to know God? Intergenerational Programming is teaching scriptural truths in interesting and lively ways so all ages will learn and apply these truths to everyday life.

Figure 3.3 is a diagram I have used often to help teachers understand the necessity of using more than their words to teach. The more action, the more learning!

Teens

Teenagers may be the toughest *or* best audience to respond, so here are a few thoughts on helping them engage in IP.

1. Gear the music toward teens' likes and ask them to help with playing or leading the music.

2. Encourage them to form a separate group if that would help them feel more comfortable.

3. Ask them to take some leadership in the program itself—teaching a lesson, leading an activity, or taking responsibility for a drama.

4. Consider offering them special roles, such as program photographer or filmmaker, setup and takedown assistant, or demonstration helper.

As a church leader, you will have some idea of what special interests your youth have, and you can also invite them to be a part of the planning for the Intergenerational Program.

Media

My bias has been to limit electronic media, particularly in camp settings. If you center your program on a film series, select these very carefully for broad age-based format. Remember that you want *active learners* rather than *passive viewers*, so balance watching with doing. And if you choose to use film clips or PowerPoint presentations, limit the length of time spent in the presentation and gear it to impact all ages.

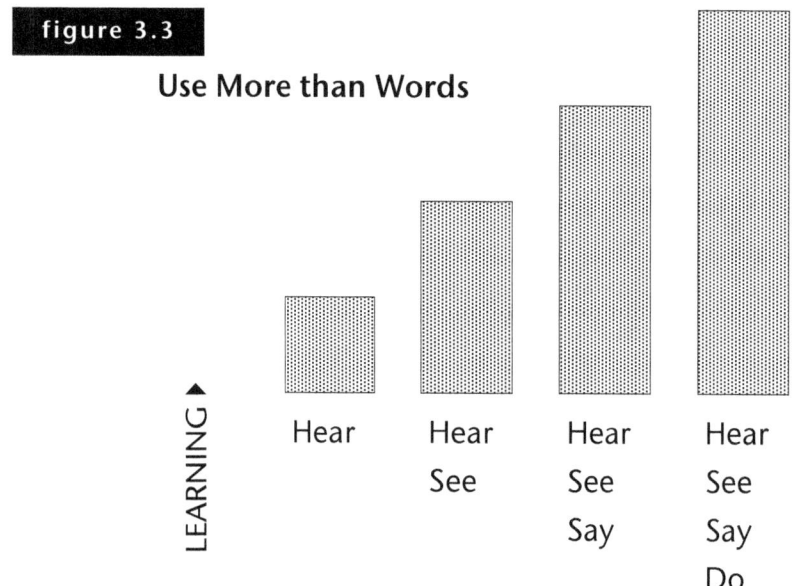

figure 3.3

Use More than Words

CHAPTER FOUR

Teach the Way Jesus Taught

How Jesus Taught—Four Teacher Styles

There are four teacher styles that, if used in a balanced way, will result in better teaching and learning. The teaching experience should be safe, stimulating, systematic, and spontaneous. Over the years, as I studied Jesus' teaching methods I saw these four styles emerge: *Safe* = kind and comforting; *Stimulating* = confronting and challenging; *Systematic* = logical and purposeful; *Spontaneous* = surprising and humorous. I have used and taught this method of teaching adults and kids for years and these qualities have been appreciated and never challenged by those I taught. Below I have illustrated aspects of these styles and explained them more fully with strategies you can use to make your teaching more effective.

A Name Game

A group of adults and children file into the fellowship hall. Coffee is brewing and snacks for later are waiting on the counter. The leader, Sharon, greets each person with a friendly smile and handshake or hug.

"Okay, everyone we are going to make two big circles." She arbitrarily divides the group approximately in half making sure little ones stay with a parent or older sibling. She directs one group to form a circle, facing outward and holding hands. She directs the second group to circle the inner group and they face inward.

"Now, we are going to play a circle name game. I want the little ones to join with a parent or another adult so you'll be one unit together. The outer circle should move clockwise and those of you in that circle should introduce yourselves with your first name and a favorite food. "Questions?" None. "Ready, go."

The four teacher styles are based on *Teach with Style: A Comprehensive System for Teaching Adults* by Jim Teeters (Redleaf Press 2001) and a program "Teach the Way Jesus Taught" developed by Jim Teeters. This system for teaching is helpful for teaching adults, kids, and intergenerational programming leadership.

The circle moves slowly and people giggle as they introduce themselves. Then Sharon tells them to continue going around but instead of telling name and favorite food, "I want you to say the name of the person across from you and his or her favorite food. This is a memory game now, but don't worry if you can't remember. We are all human!" Humorous groans, "Oh, no!" But off they go amid laughter and delight. Soon everyone knows everyone's name. Next, Sharon remixed the group and did a repeat until everyone seemed relaxed.

"Wow, I am proud of you all. Today, we are going to find out about Bible names and what some of them mean. Find a chair and let's begin!"

How Jesus Taught

Jesus was kind and caring; he listened well and showed his love as he taught. He was gentle with children and adults; he readily showed his caring concern. "Oh, Jerusalem, Jerusalem, you who kill the prophets and stone those sent to you, how often I have longed to gather your children together, as a hen gathers her chicks under her wings" (Matt. 23:37). You make it *safe* because learners need a comfortable, trust-filled learning environment in order to let go of the old and embrace the new. Learners need to let down their hair, drop their guard, and relax. That can happen when learners feel accepted and know their comfort zones are respected. Learners will take risks when judgment is suspended — that's when they will make those necessary growth-producing mistakes.

Ways to make your teaching safe:

1. Make sure the learning space is comfortable and welcoming. Share snacks, arrange chairs and other furniture to be comforting, greet people with a smile.

2. Let participants know what will be happening and how things will proceed. Have an agenda posted or have a handout explaining things. Ask for questions.

3. Help people get acquainted. If there are new folks introduce everyone, wear name tags, have get-acquainted games.

4. Strive to build trust and openness. Let people know they can opt out of activities, and encourage work in small groups. As a leader, be open yourself.

5. Keep kids safe by making sure they are well supervised and not placed in risky situations.

stimulating

Body Parts

The leader, Larry, looks over a group of kids and adults who have gathered in the sanctuary. They sit on chairs that have been moved to the tables he's placed around the perimeter. He hands out drawing paper and pens and pencils.

"Does everyone have a paper and pencil?" Little Julie raises her hand. He's missed one spot. "Here you go." And everyone is set. Larry goes to a flipchart. "Today we are going to explore our gifts and talents. I want you parents and older ones to help the little ones with this—but let them draw anything they want, in any way they want. Don't hinder the little ones. Just help them, okay?" Everyone nods.

Larry says he wants everyone to draw a picture of themselves as a part of the human body. He shows some drawings he has made. "If you are a good listener, draw yourself as an ear; if you are a hard worker and like to work with your hands, draw yourself as a hand. Everyone starts to laugh. Now does anyone have some more ideas?"

"I like to visit people in the hospital," says Pastor Marcos. "I can draw myself as a foot."

"Excellent, Pastor. Another idea?"

"I like to read and learn stuff. I can be an eyeball," says Matt, a scholarly looking teenager, and everyone laughs.

Larry gets more ideas, then invites all to start, and reminds they are to draw the body part and make it look like them. Everyone starts drawing. After everyone stops and starts to talk and laugh together, he gives these instructions:

"Okay, now I want everyone to wander around and show your drawings to anyone you want. Remember, little ones stay with a parent or older one."

After the sharing time, when everyone is seated, Larry begins to ask questions about what they thought about how everyone is so different. Eventually he begins his lesson on our unique giftedness as part of the body of Christ.

How Jesus Taught

Jesus challenged his listeners to change and grow in faith. He was often confrontational; he involved his followers in the learning process. He always got people thinking. You make it *stimulating* because learners are motivated toward positive change when they encounter ideas presented in interesting and lively ways. This style provokes and challenges learners to think, gain knowledge, change attitudes and behavior. Information is presented in ways that engage learners actively.

Ways to make your teaching stimulating:

1. Use active learning approaches. Avoid long lectures; get people moving and doing things.

2. Help participants solve real problems. Help participants identify issues and problems; help them work on solutions.

3. Challenge participants with useful ideas. Teach Bible truths that matter; make it practical.

4. Encourage creativity. Let participants invent, originate, and express in creative ways.

5. Help participants try out new learning. Help participants rehearse, practice, or teach each other new behavior and ideas.

systematic

Revelation

The group of kids and adults has gathered in the largest classroom. The leader, Julie, arranges them in a large circle around the perimeter of the room.

"This morning we are going to start our exploration of the book of Revelation. But before we begin this morning's lessons and activities, I want to hear some of what you already know about this book. The book of Revelation is full of wonderful and mysterious things—heavenly and earthly things." The group looks interested as well as puzzled. There are some newcomers in the group along with some elders and teachers.

"When I ask a question and you think you know the answer, step into the circle—I want to see what needs to be explained or explored. The little ones join with a parent; you are a unit."

"Who wrote the book? If you know, step into the circle." Four step forward and then a mother whispers to Paul, her five-year-old boy. They step forward too. "Who can say it?"

"It's John," says little Paul. Everyone applauds. Then those in the circle step back for the next question.

"Where was it written?" One older woman steps into the circle.

"It was on the island of Patmos."

Julie continues to ask questions, some more difficult and some easy. "Where in the Bible is it?" All step forward and say, "At the end." This way Julie gets to know something about the knowledge of the students she will be teaching. She also is able to identify those who may be able to assist in the teaching.

How Jesus Taught

Jesus taught with a clear aim. He was logical and purposeful and directed his teaching to the needs of his audience. In fact, his message is still meeting our needs today! You make it *systematic* because learners are more likely to change when they participate in well-planned programs. Instruction is systematic when you set shared goals, plan a program that reaches agreed-upon results and evaluates progress toward the goals. Jesus taught with a clear aim to seek and save the lost (Luke 19:10).

Ways to make your teaching systematic:

1. When possible, get participants involved in the planning. Build ownership by asking participants to help plan, and ask for feedback as you teach (even kids can tell you what they like and want).

2. Assess the participants' knowledge. Ask questions, use surveys, respond to what participants want and need to learn.

3. Have a clear aim. Be clear about what you want participants to walk away with.

4. Make your plan consistent with the aim.

5. Check to see if you are on target. Get feedback from participants, and decide how you will determine success.

spontaneous

Calling Levi

Mark is this week's lesson leader. The group has gathered and he has mixed up the participants into groups of four or five, so that some older kids are with adults other than their parents.

"Today we are going to continue to explore the calling of Levi (Mark 2:13-17) and specifically these words of Jesus: 'It is not the healthy who need a doctor, but the sick. I have not come to call the righteous but sinners.' (v. 17)." He asks each group to have a Bible open to that passage.

"I want each of your groups to come up with a skit, poem, or song to teach us *why* Jesus says this. Everyone in your group must perform the skit, poem, or song. You have ten minutes to get it together."

This is a group used to such assignments. They quickly get busy and there is an air of competitiveness in the buzzing. Soon laughter and strange song melodies emerge as they all struggle and create together.

"All right. Let's hear from this group first." Mark points to a group of four people: three older women and one six-year-old boy. They sing their song to the tune of "Jesus Loves Me."

> Jesus wants to save us sinners
> He seeks the losers not the winners
> Levi was a bad tax guy
> But Levi caught Jesus' eye
> Yes, Jesus loves me
> Yes, Jesus loves me
> Yes, Jesus loves me
> Even if I'm bad

This causes the group to break into laughter and applause. The other groups then offer their contributions, and when all have finished there is a wonderful sense of how much God cares for the lost and how we ought to be concerned for the lost too. Also, we share a sense that all of us are lost ones who are found!

How Jesus Taught

Jesus was startling and even humorous and puzzling. His stories catch us off guard. His listeners were often surprised by what he did and said: "You, who are without sin, cast the first stone," (my paraphrase from John 8:7). You make the experience *spontaneous* because learners need an opportunity and permission to try new ways of seeing. They need a new slant on things. Unpredictability fosters the process of "unfreezing" learners from the same old line of thinking. Plan and allow play, humor, and surprise in your instruction. When learners play, laugh, and take risks together, the walls of resistance weaken and fall. Jesus often was unpredictable—a camel through the eye of a needle!? His listeners were surprised at what he did and said.

Ways to make your teaching spontaneous:

1. Help participants tell their stories. Allow time for people to share unique life stories.

2. Make it funny, make it fun. Tell funny stories or let others tell theirs; get participants doing activities that are fun and make them laugh.

3. Use imagination and the arts. Have participants sing, draw, write, and perform original work; challenge participants to create.

4. Build risk taking. You want to involve the unpredictable, create surprise, and promote safe methods of self-disclosure.

5. Take time to reflect. Allow participants to be still and let the Spirit speak; let silence be a part of the teaching.

The Four Teacher Styles Balanced

The key to making these styles work is a balance of instruction as illustrated in Figure 4.1. You might note that the teacher styles form two sets of opposites: Safe is the opposite of Stimulating, and Systematic is the opposite of Spontaneous. These four styles are like forces that operate to create a more effective learning environment. You might imagine that these four styles are like the four corners of a blanket pulled tight by four people. In the middle of the blanket is a ball (effective learning). If one of the people lets go of a corner, the ball goes rolling off and onto the ground (Figure 4.2). This is how I'd like you to think of the four styles—keeping them in balance, and all in equal tension presents the "perfect storm" of a teaching environment. Naturally teachers can't be Jesus, but we can use the approaches he used!

figure 4.1

Teach the Way Jesus Taught—Four Teacher Styles

Balance the four Teacher Styles to have more lively and effective teaching as well as greater potential for learning and growing in children and adults during Intergenerational Programming.

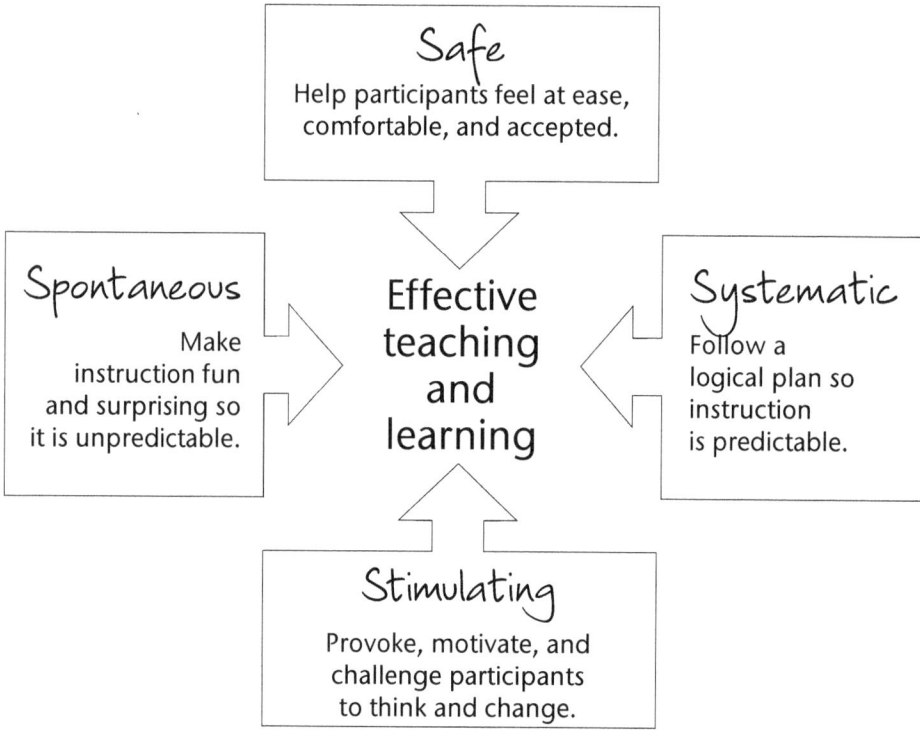

figure 4.2

Balancing the ball of learning on the blanket of the teaching environment

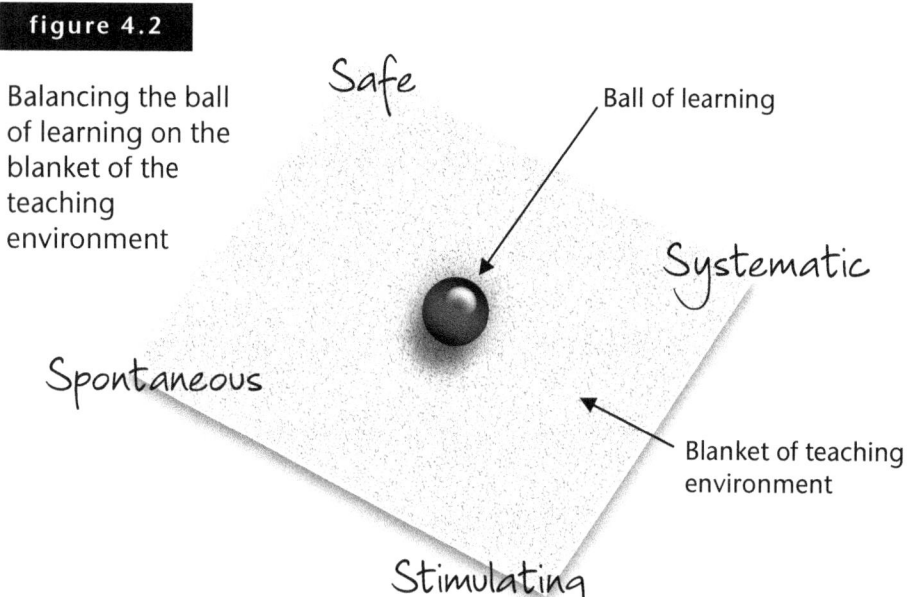

CHAPTER FIVE

Twelve Interactive Learning Methods

Interactive Teaching

The key to successful and lively teaching is the use of interactive methods that engage the learner. Below I have listed and described twelve methods using the acronym INTERACTIVES. As you plan your lesson, look over these methods and see how any one or more might fit your lesson plan.

I = Introduction Activities
N = Nature Exploration
T = Teach Each Other
E = Exchange and Discussion
R = Role playing and Dramatics
A = Action and Movement
C = Contests and Games
T = Telling Stories
I = Illustrations and Demonstrations
V = Virtual Reality and Imagination
E = Express Creativity
S = Solve Problems

Introduction Activities

Introduction and getting acquainted exercises can be used with both new groups and those who have been together awhile. There is always something new to learn about each other just by adding variety. In Resource 9, I provide a list of such warm-up activities that are easy and fun to do to open a session or to use as energizers to wake folks up.

Nature Exploration

From Genesis to Revelation, nature is used to teach wisdom and spiritual lessons. Bring in something from nature or send the class out to nature. Nature as a teacher is particularly helpful at family camps and special events. The tree of life, the uniqueness of every leaf, water, light, a field of wheat—all these bring to mind scriptural lessons. Activities that allow participants to explore, examine, discover, and then respond and discuss provide rich fodder for learning not only about God's creation, but spiritual principles.

Teach Each Other

I want to re-emphasize that when you teach something, you learn it as well. Let small groups or individuals find truth and teach it to others. Divide proverbs or parables among small groups and have them decipher the truth they reveal. Then have an exchange of teaching by each group with another group or share their discoveries with the whole group. Each group could be encouraged to demonstrate or illustrate their truth.

Exchange and Discussion

Assign discussion leaders in small groups and encourage leaders to allow kids as well as adults to get involved. Use open-ended questions so anyone can answer. Give groups a question to tackle: Why was Moses so afraid to talk? How can we be braver? Who is the bravest person you know? Get partners exchanging ideas and then they can share with other pairs. When you teach, it's best to keep it brief. Use a "lecturette"—a short, informative talk (five to seven minutes). To add power to your brief presentation, stop and have everyone do a "neighbor nudge"—a brief discussion with a partner in response to the lecturette. Participants can use this as a bridge to ask questions or give their reactions. Ask a three-year-old why Moses is afraid, and you may be surprised and enlightened! Interviewing people is an easy way to have an exchange. Provide an interview sheet or decide as a group the interview questions, then in small group start the interviews. Switch interviewer and interviewee. Everyone gets to share.

Role Play and Dramatics

Act out Scripture stories or make up plays to illustrate Bible truths. There are books of plays, but it may be more enlightening and fun for participants to create their own. In family events, dramatic presentations of Scripture stories are popular. Getting volunteers to join in and act the parts adds another dimension of interaction. Try a slow-motion drama, one with no words, or a shadow play. A fun activity for youth is filmmaking. People bring video cameras, and you can give one to each small group and then have a film festival. You can do the same thing by telling stories with slide shows from photographs in sequence. Check out these Web sites:

> http://christianplays.net
> http://www.christiancrafters.com/skits.html

Action and Movement

In a "Walk through the Bible" workshop we literally traveled around the room in the same directions the Israelites wandered toward the Promised Land. Circle games and movements offer possibilities. Having people line up along a wall to indicate their opinions or degrees of agreement with an idea is an active way for people to express themselves. In a family camp we learned about being a family by a movement activity and song called "We're Weaving a Family." The group started by holding hands, and then the leader pulled the line along, weaving under the clasped hands in and through until we were "weaved tight." "Alice the Camel" is a fun circle game with a song and is another example of using movement (see Resource 5).

Contests and Games

Grab a game book and modify the games for your teaching purposes (for example, "Simon Says" can teach the value of obedience; "Red Light/Green Light" can teach the value of listening to the Holy Spirit's prompting.) Board games can be created or modified to fit the teaching aim (land on a square and act out the Scripture truth listed). Relays, challenges, and even TV game shows can be used to teach. A Jeopardy-style quiz show with questions to fit the age of contestants is an idea. Check out these Web sites:

> http://www.gameskidsplay.net
> http://www.teacherhelp.org/christian.htm
> http://www.ultimatecampresource.com

Other resources: *Best New Games* by Dale N. LeFevre or *Everyone Wins: Cooperative Games and Activities* by Josette and Sambhava Luvmour.

Telling Stories

An activity that is fun for all ages is telling and listening to real-life stories. In small or large groups, challenge kids and adults to tell a story about certain topics that apply to the lesson (for example, snake stories, water stories, getting lost stories). Even little ones have tales to tell but an adult may need to help them focus and not ramble. Kids might do better being "interviewed" about the story they want to share. Enlist volunteers to act out the roles in a story you tell. Ask groups to create their own parables—stories that teach spiritual truths (for example, "There once was an old man who sat all alone begging for food. Along came...."). It is also fun to make up stories by letting people in small groups take turns adding to the story. Assign a theme and then let the group try to match it, each taking a turn adding to the story. Assign sound effects to groups and then have the storyteller cue them in for their sound as the story is told. Also tell Bible stories in dramatic ways or as a narrator with live action characters pulled from the audience.

Illustrations and Demonstrations

Give small groups an assignment to demonstrate a certain truth (such as joy, peace, or forgiveness) for the larger class. One example of this is when a participant teaching team asked us to imagine mixing blue and red finger paint on a paper plate. They then asked us to imagine separating the colors back to their original place. We realized that was impossible and then one teaching team member read Paul's words in Romans 8 about how nothing can separate us from the love of God in Christ. We got the message—yes, impossible! Praise God! What a demonstration. I have used the making and flying of paper airplanes to illustrate how there are some things we want to see arrive in our lives and some things we want to see depart. The related discussion focused on making changes to allow such arrivals and departures. Grab a book on scriptural object lesson ideas or check out this Web site: http://www.creativebiblestudy.com/christianobjectlesson-math1.html.

Virtual Reality and Imagination

Take a Bible scene or story and have each participant imagine he or she is one of the characters in the story. Tell how it feels to be that person. Assign each group a scenario about a problem people face, and then ask each group to try to decide what to do about it. Give several solutions. Have participants close their eyes as you tell a Bible story. Everyone imagines the scene, the smells, the sounds. Create avatars by assigning "action figures" who are real people and have their "owner" give them directions in problem situations.

Express Creativity

Involve artwork (such as drawing, coloring, sculpture, or collage). Make up songs or modify the words of songs. Write poems from prompts or group poems on a theme. Build models of Bible scenes, topical maps, altars. Create an ark, build a tower. Use photography and share pictures that teach a truth. Make journals and draw or write about what you are leaning; a group journal can become a banner or scroll. Ask participants to share their work with another person or with a small group.

Solve Problems

Write a problem on a 5x7 card and give it to a small group. When the group comes up with a solution, they can jot it on the card. Then they pass the card to the next group to add their ideas. Provide a puzzle based on the lesson (such as one using scrambled words or cardboard puzzle pieces) to individuals or groups. Send the groups on a scavenger or treasure hunt. Present quizzes to small groups to answer from Scripture. Check out this Web site: http://www.crossdaily.com/games.

Never force people to do any of the activities. Let people know they can opt out of any activity that might make them uncomfortable. Parents can demand participation of their minor children, but the program is voluntary. In my thirty-five years of experience in Intergenerational Programming, I can think of only a very few times anyone opted out except for physical disability issues. Always be aware of those with limitations and plan accordingly.

As a leader you have two choices for creating active learning in lessons. Whichever one you choose to use, the key is to get the participants actively engaged in the learning process. The following chart is a summary of these two modes (Figure 5.1). See a further explanation and example of this in Resource 3.

figure 5.1

ACTIVE LEARNING MODES
TEACHER AND LEARNER ROLES

DEDUCTION

Teacher: Instructs, demonstrates, illustrates, and/or draws out from the students the key wisdom, knowledge, or behavior that needs to be learned. This may entail use of audio-visual aids or other methods.

Learner: Listens, reads, takes notes, absorbs, contributes ideas, thinks, analyzes, imagines. The learner basically absorbs information.

Teacher: Creates experiences; gives instructions; directs activities; and encourages, guides, and/or critiques students as they make discoveries about what they learned from the explanation.

Learner: Practices, follows directions, experiments, tries out, rehearses, plays, takes risks, discovers and/or records.

INDUCTION

Teacher: Creates experiences, sets up experiments, designs activities, provides tools, and gives instructions for exploration. The activities should be designed so they naturally lead toward discoveries that help students find significant and relevant answers.

Learner: Explores, manipulates, gets involved, tries things out, immerses the self in tasks, takes risks, follows directions, keeps alert to new learning.

Teacher: Facilitates discussion, draws out truths from the exploration. The teacher helps the learner make sense out of what was experienced by bringing order out of chaos, collating information, or helping students draw conclusions.

Learner: Thinks about principles, compares, draws conclusions, ponders, makes lists, writes papers, takes notes.

Developed by Jim Teeters, MSW–Adults Teaching Adults © 1998

CHAPTER SIX

Lesson-Planning Process

Use the N. A. M. E.-Planning Process

The N. A. M. E.-Planning process is outlined in Figure 6.1 below. Follow this sequence as it is listed. In this chapter I want to walk through this process with some illustrations. I also want to incorporate the *Hook, Book,*

---

figure 6.1

The N. A. M. E.-Planning Process

N = Need of participants
    Know your participants' needs and wants.
    Ask your participants' about their needs and wants.
    Identify with your participants; how do they feel and think?

A = Aim of your lesson (What will they walk away with? That is the *Took* in your lesson plan.)
    Wisdom: What will they understand?
    Knowledge: What will they know?
    Behavior: What will they do?

M = Method to reach your aim
    Scriptural Truth: What content will you teach?
    Instructional Method: How will you affect understanding, knowledge, and/or behavior?
    Lesson Plan: What is your *Hook, Book, Look, Took* outline?
    Learning Mode: Which to use—Exploration/Explanation or Explanation/Exploration?

E = Evaluation of your lesson
    Observe your participants (Are they understanding, knowing, behaving as you had planned?)
    Ask your participants (direct questions, surveys, etc.)

Notes:
The sequence for **N. A. M. E.** must follow in the order listed above. Take enough time to know what participants want and need. This step should naturally lead you to determine your lesson aim, and the aim should naturally lead you to what and how you will teach. Be as specific as you need to in each step to design the best lesson plan to accomplish your aim. After the lesson, try to determine your success by observing or asking your participants about it.

Look, and *Took* model as well as the two *Learning Modes* to show how these all fit together.

Need of Participants

In a church, family camp, or vacation Bible school (VBS) setting you may rarely have an opportunity to get a comprehensive picture of the participants' needs or wants (if indeed, at all) before you meet them. You may have the chance to make an assessment later in the process. Make the effort if possible—this step will serve you as you plan for meeting their wants and needs. If you know the participants or are one of their members, then you will perhaps be able to identify with them or have a good picture of their learning needs and desires. Below are a few ideas for getting at needs and wants in a church setting:

3x5 card survey. Pass out cards to all who can write and ask them to write the answer to a question. (Sample: *We are planning an IP study of Job! Tell us on your card what questions you have about Job and what you want to learn.*)

Survey sheet. Pass out a survey sheet with any questions you want answered. Quick check-off questions are best, but leave room for comments.

Group interview. Gather a group representative of your participants (or as many participants as possible) and ask them questions. You can also break into smaller groups and ask questions for small group discussion—this goes for kids too.

Individual interviews. Family by family, person by person, get feedback. You can set up a table and chair in the fellowship hall or narthex, post a sign, and interview people as they come by. Another interview method is to contact people you are hoping will join the IP class and get their ideas.

Quick assessment. An assessment exercise I use often is the "I Wish…" exercise. The participants are in small groups and I ask them to identify and write on a flipchart sheet *"what* they wish to learn" and *"how* they wish to learn it." Each group reports and posts their answers for all to see and for the leader to ponder and respond. Another quick assessment is illustrated in Chapter Four in the Revelation sample lesson.

Aim of Your Lesson

Once you have some idea of what the needs and interests are, you can begin to establish the aim of your lesson or lessons. The aim includes wisdom, knowledge, and behavior. Here are some samples of aims written with the kind of wording that should help you design your lessons. I will illustrate with a lesson on the fruit of the Spirit.

- Aim for understanding. Define each of the fruits of the Spirit so you can identify them when you see them.
- Aim for knowledge. Be able to list the fruit of the Spirit in the order they are presented by Paul.
- Aim for behavior. Be able to identify *joy* in myself and others this week and note it in my "fruit journal."

Being able to articulate the aim of a lesson will naturally lead you to the methods you want to use in reaching your aim. The aim is very important; Yogi Berra once said: "If you don't know where you are going, you will wind up somewhere else." And the more specific your aim, the more you will be able to determine your success. You should be able to explain to anyone who asks why you are doing what you are doing in your IP lesson. One more note: It is good to tell your participants just what your aim is. In Larry Richards's *Hook, Book, Look,* and *Took* motif, the aim is the *Took*—it is what you want your participants to walk away with.

Method to Reach Your Aim

The method is where the proverbial rubber meets the road! You have some idea of the needs and desires of your participants, and you know your aim. Now the scriptural truths, the instructional methods, and the outline of the *Hook, Book, Look,* and *Took* will help you meet your aim. Again, let's use the fruit of the Spirit, suggested above, as our lesson. Let's design an IP lesson that will meet our aim. Below is a sample lesson:

- Aim for understanding. Define each of the fruits of the Spirit so you can identify them when you see them.
- Aim for knowledge. Be able to list the fruit of the Spirit in the order they are presented by Paul.

HOOK – Display a bowl (or several bowls around the room) of tasty fruit or fruit-flavored snacks. Play a recording of the song "The Fruit of the Spirit," or encourage the group to sing the song. <u>Alternate</u>: List types of fruit on the whiteboard and ask small groups or individuals try to match the fruits with each of the fruits of the Spirit. Have everyone share explanations for his or her ideas.

BOOK – Ask nine people to stand. Person number one starts reading, says the first fruit, and each in turn adds a fruit with person nine reading the last fruit and completing the Scripture (Gal. 5:22-23). Repeat this with other people until they can all recite it without prompting. <u>Alternate</u>: The Wave—Divide the Scripture into five sections and the participants into five groups. As you walk by, each group reads its Scripture: 1. "But the fruit of the Spirit is…" 2. "love, joy, peace…" 3. "patience, kindness, goodness…" 4. faithfulness, gentleness, and self-control…." 5. "Against such things there is no law."

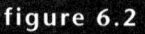

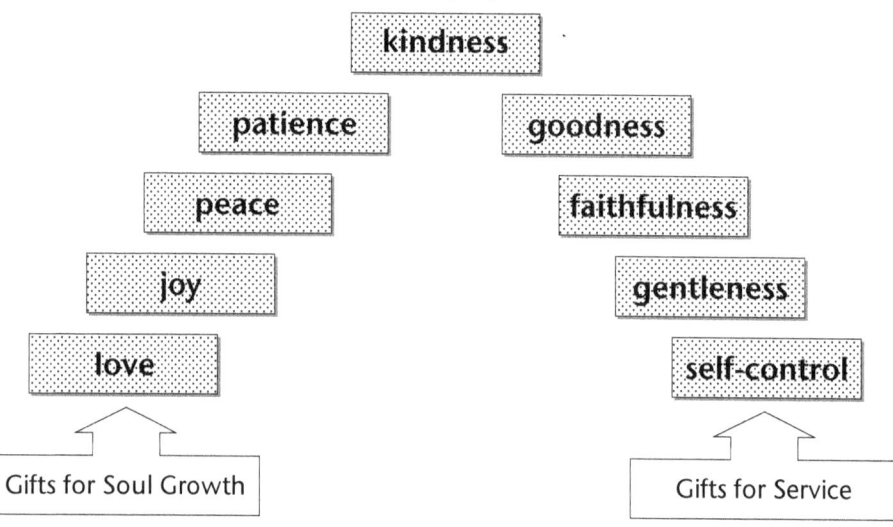

LOOK – There are two choices the for leader. Use either of these learning modes:

Explanation/Exploration

Exploration/Explanation

For the purposes of teaching and illustrating, we will let the leader design two classes, one with each learning mode:

1. Explanation/Exploration

The leader presents a chart of the Fruit of the Spirit (this could be drawn, projected, or given as a handout). See Figure 6.2.

The leader tells a story of the stairstep of the fruit—about how we collect the "gifts for soul growth," and how those lead to kindness and then to the "gifts for service." In addition, the leader gives a brief definition that fits a multi-age group (love = when a person's eyes light up when they see us, etc.) Next, she tells how this fruit is evidence of the Holy Spirit—God working in our lives. The leader then asks participants to get into small groups and briefly discuss love. The leader first requests that each person name someone who loves them or who has loved them. Next she asks each person to name one specific thing that person did to express love. Did those actions reflect fruits of the Spirit? The leader points to the right side of the fruit chart, and as she names each fruit, she asks people to indicate how those fruits were demonstrated by those who love them. If there is time, she will use other fruit from the left side and continue.

2. Exploration/Explanation

The leader has the Fruit of the Spirit chart (Figure 6.2) on a flipchart. She divides the participants into nine groups—one for each fruit. She passes around a small box with slips of paper—some colored and some white. She asks the youngest child to pick a colored slip from the box and the oldest person to pick the white one. Written on each colored slip is a different fruit of the Spirit. On each white slip is a presentation format: skit, poem, song, drawing, dance, tableau, mime, 20 questions, etc. Each group should present its fruit in its presentation format, and then ask one of the other groups to guess which fruit they are portraying. When the laughter has died down at the end of this fun experience, the leader takes the group back to the chart and asks each group to define the fruit it presented. She also asks group members to name ways the particular fruit is shown in their lives. Finally, she presents the stairstep story about both sides of the chart. (See another example of using the explanation/exploration format in Resource 3.)

TOOK – Referring back to the aim of the lesson, the leader asks everyone once more to recite the Scripture (Gal. 5:22-23) and in the time remaining she passes out the fruit to each person (and/or uses volunteers), asking each person to tell one way a specific fruit of the Spirit is demonstrated in his or her life.

Evaluation of Your Lesson

In the illustration above, the leader could use some simple ways of determining if she had accomplished the aim. This is not a school setting, so the evaluation needs to be informal and somewhat cursory. The leader did ask the group to recite the verse she was teaching. She also asked participants to name some behaviors of the fruit. She could also rotate from group to group and observe how group members responded to the lesson. In each presentation format she could observe the accuracy of how each participant defined the fruit he or she demonstrated.

The important thing is to not ignore this step. Strive to accomplish it in an effort to guide you in future lesson planning so you can enjoy continual improvement in opening up scriptural truth as you teach.

Summary

If you use the N. A. M. E.-planning process in combination with *Hook*, *Book*, *Took*, and *Look* and the *Learning Modes*, you will have an effective way to design and deliver great lessons. In the next chapter we will examine ways to put together programs in which you can insert lesson planning in a series and in different settings.

CHAPTER SEVEN

Design and Develop

Introduction

In this chapter I will list several ideas for creating interesting programs in your church, camp, or VBS. The emphasis now is how to provide ways for engaging all ages together as you design your various programs. Again, I'll explain each option and then add illustrations from real or imagined programs to help you grasp the idea. My hope is that you will "catch the vision" of each option and then create your own to fit your participants and your situation.

Where Intergenerational Programming Can Work

Intergenerational Programming (IP) can be done in a variety of ways. It can be used with small and large groups, as part of a church program, and in special events like VBS, midweek programs, retreats, or family camp. It can be a way to promote evangelism and outreach to families. If a church has a childcare program, consider offering Bible learning for all the families who use that program. You can also turn a church picnic into a fun learning event for everyone. Occasionally, the entire church education hour can be designed for all ages together. This could be an annual, quarterly, or monthly event.

Overcoming Resistance

As discussed earlier, tradition says kids and adults don't mix in church. The kiddies go off to Sunday school and the adults go off to their classes. There is also the idea that kids and adults have different developmental needs, so they should go to separate classes, learn different things. There is, of course, some truth in that, but there is also value in kids and adults learning together, as I argued in Chapter One. So how do you break with tradition to offer IP? Here are a few ideas:

- Start small. Plan a one-time IP event during the Christian education hour.
- Use this method at a family function like a picnic or potluck.
- Try it at the next family camp.

- Have a pastoral message dedicated to this concept—"let the little child come to me."
- Present the idea at a business meeting.
- Have a special orientation meeting with a potluck to discuss the idea. Be prepared to demonstrate with a short lesson.
- Demonstrate on a Sunday morning using the "fishbowl" method—a few people take part while the rest of the congregation observes.
- Demonstrate for the church leaders and their children at a special function exclusively for them.
- Try a family-night event and introduce an IP Bible learning session.
- Get this book into church leaders' hands.

The idea has to start somewhere and if you are holding this book in your hands, you may be the one to get the ball rolling. Prayerfully take the idea to the appropriate committee or leader and see what happens. Once the idea is tried, you have jumped the biggest hurdle. If it is successful and people like it, find more ways to make it happen. Soon it will become a natural addition to the Christian education offerings in your church or organization.

A Variety of Ways to Use Intergenerational Programming

IP can be integrated into the church program in several ways, such as through special events, regular CE programming, picnics, and outings. Discuss the idea in your governing body, CE committee, or elders. Someone should take charge of the IP or ask a committee to do the planning. Once an event or series is planned, a leader or coordinator should be appointed to manage the program operation and details, and delegate duties to others involved. Here are some of the areas that should be covered:

- Direction (leadership)
- Publicity
- Program
- Set-up, seating arrangement, and equipment
- Materials and supplies
- Art
- Music
- Refreshments
- Take-down and clean-up
- Evaluation and follow-up

Center of Interest

Family camps I led created unique symbols based on each lesson's Scripture passage. These various centers of interest build anticipation in the learners. Here are a few examples of such centers of interest:

- 60-foot "whale" made of black plastic sheeting, plastic pipes, and duct tape for the story of Jonah
- 8-foot plywood giant with a target hole in his head for the story of David and Goliath
- Wooden and cloth "castle" for the story of Queen Esther
- Pyramid for the story of Joseph in Egypt
- Shocks of grain for the story of Ruth
- Large mural of a multi-ethnic group for a program on the family of God
- A manger scene for the story of Mary (Christmas and beyond)
- Some collapsible walls for the story of Joshua
- Large ship-shaped structure of black plastic sheeting, plastic pipes, and duct tape for Noah's Ark
- A real or cardboard fruit tree for the creation story

Other ideas: A center of interest can include smaller items such as 5x7 cards folded in half to be "table tents," small cardboard cutouts, words, and/or pictures that represent the topic of the event. Wall hangings, posters, and other depictions help set the tone. You can be as elaborate or as simple as the budget and the creative talents of people allow. One camp I participated in had a character in costume as the center of interest—that person can greet people in a certain style or simply appear at times during the event. A piñata or special box decorated to enhance interest is also possible. Another idea is to construct the center of interest or allow it to "emerge" during the duration of the program. For example, build an altar with stones people find or bring, work on a large banner with pictures and words about the topic, or design a mural on a large, blank wall or long role of butcher paper. Participants can create the center of interest themselves, guided by clear instructions from the leader.

Music and Songs

This is a natural for any program. Pick songs to fit the theme of your program. To drive the message of the lesson home, use a theme song that people sing over and over. Another way to use music is to create new words for familiar songs, making a song that fits the lesson. An example of this is from a program on Joshua and the conquest of Jericho (Figure 7.1).

---

figure 7.1

Joshua Song
(Roughly to the tune of "Jericho")

You've heard about the courage of Esther
You've read about Abraham
You've marveled at the strength of Sampson
But Joshua was the music man, yeah
Joshua was the music man

Joshua sent the brave spies in
To check out Jericho
Rahab liked the spies a lot
So she hid them from the foe, yeah
So she hid them from the foe

Rahab helped them get away
And kept them from the sword
She lowered them out a window
With a long, strong scarlet cord, yeah
With a long, strong scarlet cord

God told Israel to cross the Jordan
They thought they would be drowned
But God piled up the water
Crossed that river on dry ground, yeah
Crossed that river on dry ground

The priests took stones from the Jordan
And built an altar high
To remind them that their mighty God
Will always get them by, yeah
He'll always get them by

The people marched 'round Jericho
Seven times around that day
And when they heard those trumpets blow
Jericho was mud and clay, yeah
Jericho's just mud and clay

Yeah, Joshua was the music man
He took Jericho with a song
And when the trumpet section played
Those walls did not last long, <u>no</u>
Those walls did not last long

Well, here's the moral of this story
My tale of course is true
If you simply trust the good Lord
He'll always pull you through, yeah
He'll always pull you through

CHORUS

Joshua fit the battle of Jericho
Jericho, Jericho
Joshua fit the battle of Jericho
And the walls came a-tumblin' down, yeah
And the walls came a-tumblin' down

Activities and Games

You can use common games like hide-and-seek, make up modified versions of common games (*group* hide-and-seek), or create your own games to match the lessons. Game books and resources on the Internet can get you started, and then you can use your imagination to add your own twist. Of course the possibilities are infinite, but I'll offer up a few examples:

- Building an altar with gathered stones, to simulate those biblical events and to stimulate a discussion of marking spiritual events in our lives.
- Building a tower with prescribed materials. Whose is the strongest against the "wind" (the leader blows on each structure to test it)?
- Making banners.
- Playing a modification of the game "Crows and Cranes." This tag game can be modified with two sides, and the "call to arms" is "Egyptians and Israelites."
- Playing a game calling for people to be guided through a maze (chairs, benches, pews). People are paired with an individual "shepherd" and through the confusion of voices each "lamb" has to listen only to the voice of its shepherd and ignore all other voices.
- Facilitating a "creation" experience in which families or groups make a sculpture, collage, or any other creation as a prelude to a discussion of our Creator God.
- Telling stories. In a "God's Water Works and Wonders" family camp, people told their "water stories" to each other in small groups. Small groups or families can think of what water creature most characterizes them.
- Playing a game of "keep the balloon from falling" to demonstrate the agony of "the fall" caused by Adam. The disappointment of "the fall" mirrors the original fall.
- Organizing a treasure hunt with small groups competing for the prize, to stimulate a discussion of "treasures in heaven."

The key is to make these activities engaging and memorable for both kids and adults and to get everyone involved in activities that open teaching opportunities. Laughter, fun *and* learning are what you want.

See Appendix 2 for some resources for games and activities you can use "out of the box" or modify for your teaching purposes.

Short, Dynamic Lessons

When you are addressing intergenerational groups, you don't want long, boring talks by leaders. Strive for short, dynamic, and engaging lessons. Object lessons and stories are important. Give each person a mustard seed to hold when you teach the "mustard seed faith." Involve the audience, especially kids, in your talk. Can they hold flashlights when you discuss "the light of the world?" Use other visual methods: charts, pictures, objects, or demonstrations to get your point across. I remember singing, "rock-and-roll" style, about Quaker simplicity: "Give me simplicity to free my soul, I want to get lost in your rock 'n role and drift away!" The crowd was laughing and learning. Teach profound lessons in ways that spark both little ones and older ones.

Drama

Presenting Scripture through drama is powerful. I remember seeing a drama about the agony of Sarah's desire but inability to have a child because of her old age. But then she did give birth and the baby in the drama was a pug (a little, ugly dog carried tenderly in a blanket by the new "mother.") We howled and laughed but never forgot the wonder of an unexpected birth! You can play it in a humorous way (as above) or realistically, word for word, right from Scripture—"If any one of you is without sin, let him be the first to throw a stone at her" (John 8:7). Drama—short or long—should definitely be a regular feature of IP lessons.

Visual Arts/Crafts

Kids like to make things and so do adults. Simple crafts are an important part of teaching and learning Bible truth. If you hear "the name of the Lord is a strong and mighty tower," what can you imagine drawing, designing, or building? If you hear "Resist the devil and he will flee from you," or "Come near to God and he will come near to you," what images come forth in your mind? Now draw that! The arts-and-crafts element can be important. Making your own "joy journal" and creating posters for remembering that "God loves me" are not only fun, they aid in learning and faith as well. If there are people in your congregation who have talents for visual arts, enlist them to help you design ways to make learning actively visual.

Movement

There is a wonderfully simple song "We're Weaving a Family" that you can sing when a large group holds hands and tangles itself into a "loving knot" as they "weave a family."

lyrics:
We're weaving a family
We join our hands together
Weave a family
Join together
Pass the caring along!

I have danced a Jewish dance, played "Alice the Camel" (see Resource 5), and I've been various animals in the ark. You can use charades and mime experiences. Moving one's body is an important part of memory and learning, and it delights kids and adults.

Another movement activity is the blessing song where the group is divided in half—one half is the inner circle and the other the outer circle. The inner circle faces out and the outer circle faces in, and as people greet each other in the rotating circles, they sing this song:

May the Spirit of God rest upon you *(hand raised in a blessing)*
May Christ's peace be yours forever more *(palms together in greeting)*
May the Spirit illuminate your heart *(place a hand on your heart)*
Now and forever more.

This provides a peaceful, quieting experience and is great for camp beginning or ending.

Costumes

Kids and adults like to dress up. Remember the Christmas costumes we've worn—the shepherds, the wise men? And don't forget that animals are a key element in the Bible—fish, lion, dove, or bear. Costumes provide an aid to imagination, and stories come alive when people or kids don costumes to create an element of realism.

Special Food

If you teach about the loaves and the fish, serve up some of that to the participants. If you are teaching about the Passover, include Passover food. In family camps we have served lamb, fish, and vegetarian meals

(Passover, loaves and fishes, and the Daniel diet!). Just think of the possibilities: milk and honey, all foods are clean (Mark 7:19), bread and wine (or grape juice), locusts (gummy bears) and wild honey.

Group Assignments

One strong and creative way you can involve your participants is to ask groups to teach a portion of the Scripture. Use clear directions, such as: Help us learn Matthew 7:24-29 (the wise and foolish builders) by deciding:

1. What important point you will teach (the aim of the lesson).

2. How you will get us doing something active (using any props or activities you can think of to make our learning fun, active, and meaningful).

3. How you will bring out the truth in a simple lesson.

I have been surprised and pleased over the years as I have watched groups of adults and kids design learning. The leader gives up some control, but creates a marvelous opportunity for others to teach and learn. Remember that teaching something immensely increases the learning of it (see Resource 4).

Theme: Arranging Scriptural Lessons

An important element of IP is creating and arranging lessons out of Scripture. ("The Story of Joseph" follows as an example.) Stories or scriptural passages can be arranged into a series of individual lessons with a central theme. A scriptural passage can also be a stand-alone lesson with its own theme. You may want to have a special IP lesson once per month, each one as a stand-alone program. Either option can serve a purpose. However, if you want to have a series of lessons on a theme, there are two ways to do that.

1. Start with a scriptural passage and then develop a theme.

2. Start with a theme and then search for relevant scriptural passages.

The Story of Joseph
(Genesis, chapters 37; 39—45)

"We decided on the story of Joseph. Any ideas for our theme?" The leader searched the faces of the program committee.

"Well, Joseph was involved in both deceptions and truth telling."

"Yes, and also dreams were an important part—Joseph's dream, the baker's dream, and Pharaoh's dreams."

"And the cupbearer's dream."

"Well, that is true. But look at the deceptions: The brothers sell him and lie to the father; Potiphar's wife deceived Joseph; and Joseph deceived his brothers." Several nodded their heads in agreement.

"Hey, what if we named our series, 'Dreams and Deceptions: The Story of Joseph'?"

"Amen!" Everyone joined the declaration.

"What are the lessons?" The group waded into the Scripture again and came out with these notes on lesson ideas for their next meeting.

- **Family Traditions** — How Joseph, his father, and his brothers related. A little history of Jacob and his sons. We'll invite families and groups to make a family "traditions crest." Teach the importance of traditions.

- **Joseph's Dreams and His Brothers' Anger** — The lesson can center on pride and humility, how pride gets us all into trouble. Also, the intrigue of dreams and how they play a part in our own lives. We can have a pantomime of the dreams, maybe a "shadow show." Also, we can have people tell their dreams.

- **Revenge in the Field** — Our first look at deception. This would be an exciting drama. Also, a game of hide-and-seek where groups hide one of their members and everyone has to go looking—"Where Is Joseph" game. Kids will love that. This could open up the idea of how God can take even a bad thing and turn it to good. When have we felt something was bad and God made it good?

- **Potiphar's House** — Here is the second deception and a good drama. With kids it needs to be tempered, maybe as a melodrama, humorous and overplayed. We learn how honesty is sometimes not rewarded in the short run.

- **Joseph in Prison** – More dreams and great drama with Joseph interpreting the dreams. The cupbearer and the baker both have dreams, then Pharaoh has a dream. These could be great for group drawings. Maybe this could be told in storyteller format. Ask Marge, she's a good story teller—she'd do it! Then we'll pair kids and adults to create pictures of these dreams and display them. Here we see how God is working things out.

- **Joseph Becomes Great and the Famine Occurs** – There is a lesson here about saving, being frugal. Big lesson on the providence of God.

- **Joseph Confronts His Brothers** – Deception again, but they were being punished and forgiven all at once. Here is another great drama. The reconciliation and forgiveness is powerful and should be the most important part of the lesson. In silence everyone could forgive people who have betrayed or hurt them. This could follow a very moving drama.

- **Celebration** – Let's have a party! We are celebrating how God works, how God loves, how God forgives, and how we can reconcile and find peace.

At the next meeting the group made more detailed plans and set aims for each lesson. They decided on The Coat of Many Colors as the center of interest and decided to have a few posters of Egypt put up all around the church each time they had the lessons. Norma and Alex volunteered to sew a coat of many colors for the pastor to wear on the lesson days.

Program-Planning Process

Here is an overview of the planning process:

- Decide the scriptural passage, theme, and a catchy title.
- Arrange the lessons within the program.
- Conceptualize the lessons and activities to fit the ages of participants.
- Decide which program options to use as outlined above.
- Develop the program outline and program schedule (see "Twenty Sample Programs" section).
- Develop a guide sheet for all the leaders—the format, assignments, etc.
- Publicize the program to your target audience.
- Launch the program, and explain the IP format to participants.

Resources

resource 1

Twenty Sample Intergenerational Programs

In this section you will find ten Old Testament sample programs and ten New Testament sample programs that you can take and use for the Christian education hour in your church. In addition, there are fourteen series of related programs that can be used to plan the curriculum for family camps or for the Christian education hour. Altogether there are ninety-five individual sample programs and individual programs suggested in the outline series.

Sample Programs: Old Testament

lesson 1

The Fall

Aim: Be reminded of how we all tend to reach for the forbidden things, and that there are consequences when we do. It is best to stay true to the Lord's call on your life.

Theme: Yes, we do sin and "fall," but Jesus died for us and he replaces Adam and Eve's curse with his marvelous saving love.

HOOK ▶ a. A snake display.
b. Fake snake a leader holds.
c. A leader shows two items: carrot sticks (okay to munch on) and candy (forbidden for the time being); the leader asks people to guess what today's lesson is about.

BOOK ▶ Genesis 2 and 3. The leader can tell the story and emphasize 2:15-17 and 3:1-13 (14-25 — use the curses based on the audience). The consequences included being barred from the "tree of life." This is a foreshadowing of the cross, which brings us back to life!

LOOK ▶ Explanation/Exploration: The leader tells the story in a dramatic way and explains each of the elements:

1. The fruit that was forbidden (like the candy dish) (Gen. 2:15-17).

2. The snake, which is Satan, who wants to accuse and trick us into doing the wrong things (we do battle with the evil side daily) (Gen. 3:1-3).

3. The temptation (Gen. 3:4-7).

4. The confrontation with God (Gen. 3:8-13).

Next, the group is divided into these three groups who look over their Scripture and then present a skit to go along with it. The group selects its actors and actresses, and could include a narrator, Adam, Eve, God, Satan, tree, fruit, or any element in the Scripture. The plays are presented. After the plays, the leader reads the consequences or summarizes them in a dramatic way — now you know why you have to mow the lawn, why snakes crawl, why women go to a hospital for birth, why we have to work hard, and why we turn into dust!

TOOK ▶ Each group creates a prayer for the whole group to remind us of our temptations and the need to stay true to God's plan for our lives and to enjoy the life-giving salvation and Spirit of God. Example: "Lord, help us remember to be thankful for your life-giving love. Help us to make right choices." The leader can then remove the "forbidden" sign and share both fruit and candy!

Center of Interest ▶ a. Snake;

b. Fruit (sign that says "good for you"), and next to it a bowl of candy (sign that says "forbidden — temporarily").

lesson 2

Escape with Noah

Aim: Discover what pleases and displeases God.

Theme: The story of Noah and the ark is a classic. It is about those who reject God and one man and his immediate family who find favor with God. God saves them from catastrophe through Noah, who listens and obeys God. The story is a foreshadowing of the Savior who is perfect and faithful. Of course, Noah is not perfectly faithful like Jesus.

HOOK ▶ a. A tub of water, little boats (made by participants) placed in the water.
b. A group boat designed and floated.
c. Boat stories (pleasant and dangerous).
d. Boat-design contest (see whose can float the longest when weighted with pennies).
e. Form a boat out of people, with kids inside the outline, and move the whole boat around.

BOOK ▶ Gen. 6–9.
Give a brief synopsis of the story—"Let me tell you about a man who pleased God when others did not…."

LOOK ▶ Exploration/Explanation: Watch a drama of Noah or listen to a dramatic reading. This can be humorous, or serious and poignant. Next, ask groups to make two lists: what pleases God and what displeases God. Ask the group to imagine how behavior displeasing to God gets us in a *flood* of troubles.

Explanation/Exploration: Ask groups to make two lists: what pleases God and what displeases God. Ask the group to imagine how behaviors displeasing to God get us in a flood of troubles. Next, watch a drama of Noah or listen to a dramatic reading (humorous, or serious and poignant).

TOOK ▶ Ask everyone to list or think of things they do that displease and please God. Then challenge everyone to eliminate one thing they do that displeases God and do more of what pleases God this week.

Center of Interest ▶ A boat made of black sheeting and pipe, a canoe or rubber raft, a large boat and trailer in the parking lot, miscellaneous materials provided for the group to build a boat (e.g. let it rain confetti).

lesson 3

Cast Jonah Overboard

Aim: Remember to do what God tells you to do sooner, rather than later.

Theme: The story of Jonah presents someone who did not want to do what God told him to do. He experiences the consequences of disobedience and gets it right, somewhat. The story shows the consequences of disobedience and God's grace for even those who are rebellious. It foreshadows the mercy of God, shown by Christ.

HOOK ▶ a. Human ship race—groups hold hands and maneuver through a maze (did we lose anyone?).
b. Any of the activities related to Noah, mentioned previously.
c. List of people we wish God would punish (would we tell them of God's love for them?).

BOOK ▶ Jonah (whole book)
a. Present Jonah in a drama.
b. Tell the story and then read Jonah's prayer in the whale.

LOOK ▶ Exploration/Explanation: Divide the participants into two groups. One group carries a sign with the words "Bad People" (or they may be wrapped in crime-scene ribbon). The other group carries a sign that says "God Is Love," and goes over and releases the first group. The two groups join together and sing "1 John 4:7 and 8." Next reverse the groups and the signs, and repeat. Give a short talk about Jonah not showing the mercy that God desires. Ask the group to give examples from their lives.

Explanation/Exploration: Give a short talk about Jonah not showing the mercy that God desires. Ask the group to give examples from their lives.

Next, divide the participants into two groups. One group is given a sign with the words "Bad People" (or they may be wrapped in crime-scene ribbon). The other group, carrying a sign that says "God Is Love" goes over and releases the first group and the two groups join together. Next reverse the groups and the signs, and repeat.

TOOK ▶ Sing: "Oh, How He Loves You and Me" then ask the group to think of someone they need to love this week.

Center of Interest ▶ A whale made out of black plastic sheeting and plastic pipe, a large photo of a whale or fish, inflatable whale, a papier-mache fish made as a group project.

lesson 4

David Is Chosen King—the Lord Sees the Heart

Aim: Understand that God looks at your heart, not at how good you look in the world's eyes.

Theme: This is the story of how David, the youngest son of Jesse, is selected by God and anointed by Samuel to be king of Israel. We learn how God looks upon the heart of David, a mere boy, over the older sons of Jesse.

HOOK ▶ a. Enlist the services of a sheep.
b. Have everyone draw a sheep on a large butcher-paper mural.
c. Give everyone a small vial of oil for anointing each other.
d. Give everyone a heart-shaped candy.
e. As people enter, ask them to write their name on a big paper heart.

BOOK ▶ 1 Samuel 16.
a. Tell the story;
b. present a drama;
c. present a dramatic reading of the story.

LOOK ▶ Exploration/Explanation: Make a list of all the things that make someone popular and famous in the world or in our society. Make another list of those things that God cares about in our lives. Next, review the story of David being chosen over the older, more experienced brothers. Ask why God chose David.

Explanation/Exploration: Review the story of David being chosen over the older, more experienced brothers. Ask why God chose David. Next, make a list of all the things that make someone popular and famous in the world or in our society. Make another list of those things that God cares about in our lives. Put each word or phrase on cards. On a big heart, put the cards with worldly items around the outside of the heart and the cards with things God cares about inside the heart.

Option: Play a game of "Simon Says" but call it "Shepherd Says" to introduce the role of shepherd. People identify the qualities of someone selected to be the leader in the game (quick, has leadership skills, sharp-eyed, knows the rules, etc.)

TOOK ▶ Use oil to anoint each person as a servant of God. Use this prayer: "May God bless you with a great and important thing to do for God and people." Option: Each person can say or read the prayer and anoint another person. Young or old can anoint.

Center of Interest ▶ Sheep or lamb, person dressed as shepherd, large cardboard cutout of a sheep.

lesson 5

Ask for Wisdom

Aim: Learn to desire wisdom. Explore wisdom and how valuable it is compared to treasures on earth. Discover where wisdom comes from.

Theme: When, in a dream, God told Solomon to ask for anything, Solomon asked for wisdom. Because Solomon asked for wisdom and not worldly things, God blessed him.

HOOK ▶ A treasure chest where people can pick a card with a wise choice (love, joy, peace, etc.) written on one side and a worldly item (new car, bike, $1,000, etc.) on the other side. Ask which they would choose. This is a "tickler" for showing the temptation the world confronts us with. b. The cards can have pictures instead of words.

BOOK ▶ 1 Kings 3:5-15.
Present a dramatic reading of this Scripture. Define *wisdom* for all ages as: "Listening to God and doing what God wants you to do."

LOOK ▶ Exploration/Explanation: Ask the group to pretend they can have anything they ask for. Tell them to be as selfish as they can and ask for anything they want.

Groups come up with a list (or draw all items on a poster). Present this in a humorous way, allowing freedom to be "selfish." Next, on the other side of the paper, list (or draw) some things the wisest people might desire most. Retell the story and emphasize how we can all ask for wisdom, which results in being blessed by a loving God. See definition above.

TOOK ▶ End the session with the circle movement: Use the movement and blessing song where the group is divided in half—one half is the inner circle and the other the outer circle. The inner circle faces out and the outer circle faces in, and as people greet each other in the rotating circles, they sing or say this blessing:

May the wisdom of God rest upon you
(hand raised in a blessing)
May Christ's peace be yours forever more
(palms together in greeting)
May the Spirit illuminate your heart *(hand placed on the other person's heart)*
Now and forever more
(move to the next person).

This provides a peaceful, quieting experience that focuses on the gifts we receive from a loving God.

Center of Interest ▶ Treasure chest, cardboard crowns, proverb posters taped to walls.

lesson 6

What Pleases God?

Aim: Learn what God wants from his people. God doesn't need sacrifice, but instead God wants us to be thankful, be honest, pray to him in times of trouble, and listen to and obey his teaching.

Theme: Taking portions of Psalm 50, we learn that God is calling us and blessing us as we become thankful, honest, prayerful, and obedient.

HOOK ▶ Have everyone form a circle or line up and work together to memorize Psalm 50:14-15 with "the wave" motion. Here are suggested portions (from CEV but you may want to use another version or different portions):

1. *I am God the most high!*
2. *The only sacrifice [or substitute "gift"] I want...*
3. *is for you to be thankful...*
4. *and to keep your word.*
5. *Pray to me in time of trouble.*
6. *I will rescue you,*
7. *and you will honor me.*
8. *Psalm 50:14-15*

BOOK ▶ Psalm 50 (Particularly verses 1, 10-15, 23). Read the Scripture.

LOOK ▶ Explanation/Exploration: Read over the Scripture and explain how God does not need anything from us because God owns it all. Ask participants to name all the things (animals or objects) that God owns. Ask: What can we give to God that God doesn't have already? Reread the Scripture and encourage participants individually or in small work groups to list those things God desires (such as being thankful, keeping your word, praying in times of trouble, being obedient).

Next, working in pairs (an older person and a younger person), write or draw on a card, or make clay or play-dough versions of these true gifts we can bring. Provide small boxes and ask people to put their "gifts" in a box and gift wrap it. Share it with another pair, who will open it.

TOOK ▶ Summarize how God wants our hearts, our obedience, our gifts of thankfulness and prayers. Encourage people to take the gifts home and place them somewhere to remind them of what God wants.

Center of Interest ▶ A huge gift wrapped box; wrapping paper and ribbon and little boxes; a Christmas tree (artificial if out of season).

Sports fans will be familiar with "the wave." A cheerleader runs along in front of the crowd and people in the sections of the grandstands rise up as the cheerleader passes and yell with their hands up so the crowd looks like a wave. In "the wave" Scripture memorization, divide the group into sections and ask each section to say a portion of the Scripture in turn. Keep rotating the sections so everyone eventually repeats the Scripture over and over. For more excitement, have each section stand up and/or raise their hands as they recite.

lesson 7

A Strong and Mighty Tower

Aim: Remember that God is our strength, and as we follow God's ways we can run to him and he will shelter us. God is our protection!

Theme: Provide a dramatic way to draw attention to God as our mighty tower and refuge. He is there—strong, protective, and ready to help—whenever we need him.

HOOK ▶ a. Song: "The Name of the Lord." Make up motions or invite the group to suggest motions for the song.
b. Ask participants to name the tallest towers they have seen.

> The name of the Lord
> Is a strong and mighty tower.
> The name of the Lord
> Is a refuge for my soul.
> The name of the Lord
> Is a pillar I can lean on.
> The righteous run into
> The name of the Lord.
> The righteous run into
> The name of the Lord.

BOOK ▶ Proverbs 18:10

LOOK ▶ Exploration/Explanation: Have enough material available for each small group (four to five people) to make a table-top tower (see instructions below). Next, read the Scripture again or sing the song. Tell about towers of ancient times. Discuss: How do we run into the tower? Who are the righteous? How is God like a tower? How does God protect us?

Explanation/Exploration: Begin with the Scripture and song. Tell about towers of ancient times. Discuss: How do we run into the tower? Who are the righteous? How is God like a tower? How does God protect us? Next, have enough material available for each small group (four to five people) to make a table-top tower (see instructions below).

TOOK ▶ Take time for group prayers for this coming week. Pray for us to remember how strong God is, and pray to be ready (righteous) to run into him if there is any trouble ahead.

Center of Interest ▶ A picture of a strong and mighty tower (or a series of pictures).

Build a table-top tower

Object: Test to see which tower is highest and strongest when the teacher blows on them.

3 minutes to plan (members should not start until the leader gives the sign)

5 minutes to build (all members must take part)

- use all the materials
- tower must be free-standing and breeze resistant

MATERIALS
(for each tower)
10 sheets of paper
4 paper plates
2 paper cups
4 straws
4 playing cards
3 feet of masking tape
1 pair of scissors

lesson 8

The Steadfast Love of the Lord

Aim: Find solace in the truth that God loves us and his mercies are new every morning.

Theme: It is a day-by-day life we lead, trusting God. God's mercies never come to an end. Even in the midst of Lamentations we discover the mercies of God!

HOOK ▶ a. Sing "The Steadfast Love."

The steadfast love of the Lord never ceases
His mercies never come to an end
They are new every morning
New every morning.
Great is Thy faithfulness, O Lord.
Great is Thy faithfulness.

b. Play this YouTube video (http://www.youtube.com/watch?v=doFoc_FK-Uc) or another version.

BOOK ▶ Read or paraphrase Lamentations 3:19-26 and emphasize how God's compassion and mercy are new *every* morning.

LOOK ▶ Explanation/Exploration: Go over this portion of Scripture to bring to mind these points: We remember our troubles, but we remember our hope in God's great love, compassion, and faithfulness; it is good to wait quietly for all of these blessings. Use illustrations or stories for these points:

1. Troubles: What are they, who has examples?
2. Hope: What is this, what does it mean?
3. Love, compassion, mercy: What are these?
4. Waiting quietly: What is that and how do we do it?

Next, create small groups. Direct each group to come up with a song, skit, poem, or drawing for one of the following (provide materials as needed):

1. Troubles: What kind of troubles do we have?
2. Hope: What does it mean to hope?
3. Steadfast love: What is that like coming from God?
4. Waiting quietly: How do we do that?

Give groups ten minutes to prepare, and then have each group share or perform for the whole group.

Option: Each person can draw a sunrise to take home to remind himself or herself of God's mercies that are new every morning.

TOOK ▶ Sing again: "The Steadfast Love." Bring to mind that each day, when the sun comes up, you can trust again for the mercies of God. As Jesus says, "In this world you will have trouble. But take heart! I have overcome the world" (John 16:33). Give all participants a birthday card to put by their bed to remind them that each day is like a birthday—new troubles and new mercies.

Center of Interest ▶ Picture of the sunrise; bed and alarm clock, or just an alarm clock that goes off right as you start the lesson; humorous birthday cards.

lesson 9

I'm Not Mine

Aim: Be reminded of the gospel: Jesus as Savior was prophesied by Isaiah, who told how Jesus would suffer and die in our place. Jesus is our Savior.

Theme: We were "bought with blood" when Jesus died for us and took on our sins so that we would be perfect in God's eyes. We learn from John 3:16-17 that we have eternal life because God gave his Son. Also, the law was given by Moses, but Jesus Christ brought us undeserved kindness and truth.

HOOK ▶ Songs: a. "Jesus Loves Me" (little ones, oldest ones, teenage ones, disabled ones, etc. *to him belong!*);
b. "Jesus, I'm Not Mine":
Jesus, I'm not mine
Jesus, I'm not mine
I've been bought with blood
Jesus, I am thine!

BOOK ▶ Isaiah 53 (especially verses 5 and 6). Speak about this Scripture foretelling Jesus' suffering and death, and how he died so we can face God and live our lives victoriously.

LOOK ▶ Exploration/Explanation: Isaiah is interviewed, with additional questions from the audience. The focus is on Isaiah 53 and could proceed like this (in the vein of "The Thousand Year Old Man" portrayed by Mel Brooks):

"We have a special guest with us today. He has traveled not only a long distance, but he has traveled through time to answer our questions." (Isaiah appears, dressed in a Bible costume; he wipes his brow, blinks and looks around.)

"Ha!" Isaiah says, "I predicted this might happen!"

Begin to interview Isaiah and then invite the audience to ask questions. Give out questions to people to ask, if needed depending on the group. After the questions, ask if anyone has a comment. Sum up the lesson by completing any points about the remarkable parallel of Isaiah's and Jesus' mission. "How did you know this, Isaiah?" He answers: "I listen to God, very carefully!"

TOOK ▶ Ask if anyone wants to take a step toward God or wants to claim the victory over sin that Jesus offers. Also, you may want to pray a salvation prayer and invite people to quietly pray that prayer, and then tell someone about their "decision."

Center of Interest ▶ Picture of Jesus on the cross.

lesson 10
God Sings over You!

Aim: Be encouraged about how God sees us and loves us.

Theme: Here is a powerful Scripture from Zephaniah that we can remember and recite as a way of reminding ourselves how much God cares and celebrates over his people—over you and me!

HOOK ▶ Use "the wave" (see Lesson 6) to memorize this verse: Zephaniah 3:17:

1. The Lord your God is with you,
2. he is mighty to save.
3. He will take great delight in you,
4. he will quiet you with his love,
5 he will rejoice over you with singing.

BOOK ▶ Zephaniah 3:17. Have a couple of people volunteer to recite the Scripture from memory.

LOOK ▶ Exploration/Explanation: Introduce a Scripture recitation challenge. Explain that we are going to demonstrate, in a small way, how God celebrates over us. Instruct everyone in a cheer, applause, and a song to follow each person's attempt at the recitation. In other words, whether a person gets it right or wrong, the group will "take great delight" in him or her. Challenge everyone to recite the Scripture. Then follow it with this:

1. Applause and cheering!
2. Sing: "Oh, How He Loves You and Me" or "I Love You with the Love of the Lord."
3. Applause and cheering!

After all this fun, tell everyone this is just a very puny example of how God celebrates and rejoices over us. Say: "The Lord also 'quiets you with his love.'" At this point, have everyone get as quiet as they can for one minute. At the end, lead the group in the song one more time and then end with big applause and cheering!

TOOK ▶ Ask everyone to stand when you ask "Who does God take great delight in?" and "Who does God rejoice over?"

Center of Interest ▶ Several pictures of Jesus with children or of Jesus healing people; a print of the painting "Forgiven" by Thomas Blackshear.

Sample Programs: New Testament

lesson 11

Who Is My Neighbor?

Aim: Remember that the key to the kingdom is found in love for others—even love of our enemies.

Theme: Here we find the religious people unresponsive to a hurting person, and someone we think is the worst person becomes the most loving of all. We need to put aside our prejudices and just love and give of ourselves wherever there is a need. We are the neighbor!

HOOK ▶ Arrange for someone to lie on the floor as people arrive. What will happen?

BOOK ▶ Luke 10:25-37

LOOK ▶ Explanation/Exploration: There are three responses to this situation:

1. The Robbers—what's yours is mine.

2. The Priest and Levite—what's yours is yours, what's mine is mine.

3. The Samaritan—what's mine is yours.

Someone who is destined for eternal life will be like the Samaritan, "what's mine is yours." It is important to note that we don't earn eternal life; we respond to God's love by loving others—being the neighbor to them! Jesus said to find eternal life we must "go and do likewise."

Next, read the Scripture dramatically and recruit participants to act it out during the reading. Actors and actresses: expert in the law, Jesus, the man, the robbers, the priest, the Levite, the Samaritan.

Option: In small groups have people imagine who might be the "Samaritan" in our culture; who are the lowest and the ones we tend to look down on? Jesus made it plain that love can come from the most unexpected places. Make a list of those we might need to help. What does it mean to be a neighbor to them?

TOOK ▶ Remind the group: Remember, *you* are the neighbor! Go and do likewise.

Center of Interest ▶ Person lying on the floor. When someone walks up to the person he or she raises a sign that says, "Are you a good Samaritan?"

lesson 12

Rejoicing in Heaven

Aim: Be reminded that there is great rejoicing in heaven when a lost one is found. Care for the lost ones.

Theme: Jesus is being criticized for being friendly with sinners and even eating with them. We like to hang out with the "good people," but we learn there is great rejoicing when the "bad people" find their way to God.

HOOK ▶ Small groups share how they got "found."

BOOK ▶ Luke 15:1-7.
Read the Scripture or dramatize it (actors and actresses: sinners, Pharisees, Jesus, sheep, shepherd, angels rejoicing).

LOOK ▶ Explanation/Exploration: Spend some time asking questions in small groups or in the larger group such as: Who might be the sinners? Who are the tax collectors and why are they so bad? Why would the Pharisees (the religious leaders) be so mad at Jesus? Why does God want to save sinners? What happens when you lose something? How do you celebrate when you find something you've lost? Next, play a game of hide-and-seek, or hide some object (stuffed toy sheep, for example). When someone finds it everyone sings, applauds, and cheers, and treats are passed around. Repeat this for as long as time allows.

Conclude with a talk about being messengers of the gospel to those who don't know the wonderful grace of Jesus.

TOOK ▶ Challenge everyone to speak to someone this next week about being found and about how God loves that person.

Center of Interest ▶ Real sheep, stuffed toy sheep, person dressed like a shepherd with shepherd's staff.

lesson 13

Increase Our Faith

Aim: Realize that your small faith is enough. Just use it!

Theme: When Jesus' apostles said "increase our faith," Jesus said if they had faith the size of a mustard seed, they could tell a mulberry bush to go plant itself into the sea. His humor demands our attention because it teaches us not to be concerned about our faith. We have enough.

HOOK ▶ a. Put mustard seeds in a dish and try to pick up just one.
b. Guess how many mustard seeds are in a tiny glass container (prize for the closest).
c. Pass around a dish of mustard seeds and ask each person to take one and hold onto his or her seed during the rest of the class.

BOOK ▶ Read Luke 17:5-6.
If you want, include verses 1-4 as a set-up for this Scripture (asking apostles to forgive someone who mistreats them seven times in a day but apologizes). You can also ask: "How much faith does it take to do the impossible?" Then read Jesus' answer.

LOOK ▶ Exploration/Explanation:
a. Use the "Game Song" (at bottom left) or make up verses that teach about prayer. b. Draw pictures of this story in comic-book form, including the mulberry tree flying to the sea. c. Ask people to line up according to how much faith they think they have—little faith on the left and greater faith on the right. Discuss why they lined up that way.

Discussion topics:
a. In small groups show and talk about "how big is big, how small is small."
b. Jesus is using a metaphor (funny story) to answer his apostles. What do you think the metaphor means?

This Is the Way We Show Our Faith

(Tune: Here We Go 'Round the Mulberry Bush)

This is the way we show our faith
Show our faith, show our faith
This the way we show are faith
Every moment we're living.

This is the way we help the poor
Help the poor, help the poor
This is the way we help the poor
Every moment we're living.

This is the way we love each other
Love each other, love each other
This is the way we love each other
Every moment we're living.

This is the way we share our faith
Share our faith, share our faith
This is the way we share our faith
Every moment we're living.

RESOURCES **63**

lesson 14
Who Is Justified?

c. Why do the disciples think they need more faith?

d. Think of someone who you think has great faith. What makes it great?

TOOK ▶ a. Write on a 3x5 card an "impossible thing" you want to pray about. Collect and pass out the cards to others and have each one pray for that person's need. b. Have a prayer circle and pray about some need while holding a mustard seed.

Center of Interest ▶ Mustard seeds, mulberry bush (drawing, picture, or real).

NOTE: Perhaps the message is that faith is not getting God to be obedient to us, but for us to be obedient to God. Sending a mulberry bush to the sea has no meaning, but listening to God and doing what God says is truly a mark of great faith!

Aim: Understand that God is pleased when we honestly confess our sins and weaknesses.

Theme: Here we see that pride and self-righteousness are not what God wants from us. We learn that humility results in exaltation, but self-exaltation results in spiritual defeat in God's kingdom.

HOOK ▶ St. Peter and Jesus in costume greet people.

BOOK ▶ Luke 18:9-14

LOOK ▶ Exploration/Explanation: Enlist volunteers to put on the play "Elevator to Judgment" (see Resource 6).

Ask small groups to discuss this and respond to the question: "What does God want us to do?"

TOOK ▶ Offer a prayer of forgiveness for all the wrongs we have done, or group participants as prayer partners who pray this prayer together.

Center of Interest ▶ "Elevator to Judgement," actors and actresses in costume.

lesson 15

Sheep and Goats

Aim: To realize where our money and actions should go.

Theme: This is most likely the most ignored but most challenging of images that Jesus presents. We immediately realize we are goats and have nothing to rely on except the mercy and grace of Christ. We are also reminded to get busy and become servants.

HOOK ▶ Divide the room in half with two rows of chairs facing each other. As members arrive, ask them to seat themselves in either section. When all are seated, read dramatically Matthew 25:31-32. Without saying which side is which, tell people to reseat themselves.

BOOK ▶ Matthew 25:31-46. Read or have a dramatic presentation.

LOOK ▶ Explanation/Exploration: a. Write a list of the six categories of people on a flipchart: hungry, thirsty, stranger, needing clothes, sick, and in jail. Arrange participants in small groups and assign one category to each group. Ask groups to think of ways individuals or the church could reach out to their category of people. Next have each group come up with a skit that shows how this could happen, and/or how the need is not being met. The skits can show how we respond *before* and *after* we have Christ in our hearts. Each group then performs a skit.

Emphasize the importance of responding to people in need. It could have eternal consequences!

You may want to bring a list of organizations that are helping these categories of people in your own community. Display this list, or pass out copies.

TOOK ▶ If people are interested in responding to Christ's call, they can meet together to decide on a ministry to one of the categories of need. Consider both short-term and long-term responses.

Center of
Interest ▶ Sheep and goats (real, photos, drawings, etc.); sing "Make Me a Servant."

lesson 16

Fertile Soil

Aim: Discover at least one thing that will help us to become "fertile soil" for the kingdom seed.

Theme: The seed is a common metaphor in Scripture. It is something small that results in something large. In this parable we are the soil that accepts the seed, and if we are fertile ground something important will grow from our lives.

HOOK ▶ Each person responds to "What is your experience with planting a garden, as a child or as an adult?"

BOOK ▶ Mathew 13:3-9. Briefly tell the story of the sower.

LOOK ▶ Exploration/Explanation: Designate groups to represent the path, the rocky soil, the thorns, and the good soil. Call a "sower" to the front of the class. Proceed to follow along and act out the Scripture as it is read (combine Matt. 13:3-9 and 18-23, see Resource 7). Each person acts out whatever he or she feels goes along with the Scripture that is read. Form small groups. Each group gets a marker and paper. Each group discusses what they think makes us "good soil." Then the group attempts to formulate their ideas into one word and into one picture that encapsulates the idea. They then draw the picture and write the word on the paper. Each group then holds up their paper in turn and explains their response.

TOOK ▶ Ask participants to get silent and select one word from the posters that would be a good theme in their lives, and ask them to make a pact to apply it consistently during the following week. (Partners could call each other during the week to see how each is doing.)

Center of
Interest ▶ Shocks of wheat, packets of seeds given as people enter.

lesson 17

Be Doers of the Word

Aim: Recognize that believing and hearing are not as important as doing what you believe and hear.

Theme: The message of the wise builder is simple: Do what God says! We do a lot of hearing in church, but the true Christ follower acts on what he or she hears God saying.

HOOK ▶ Give everyone a rock or brick and a marking pen. Tell them to write their name, or draw a picture of themselves on one side of the rock or brick.

BOOK ▶ Mathew 7:24-27.
Read this parable or create a drama of it.

LOOK ▶ Explanation/Exploration: Reread the Scripture and ask: What does the house on sand signify? What does the house built on rock signify? In small groups participants can discuss what they have heard taught in church and what they should *do* about those teachings. Report to the whole group your findings.

Activity: Give groups building materials (sticks, blocks, etc.) and see who can build a strong structure that can hold up someone's shoe or a similar object. Let people figure out that a strong foundation is important!

TOOK ▶ On the other side of your rock or brick, write or draw something you will *do* that you heard in church or learned from Bible lessons.

Center of
Interest ▶ Cement blocks, large stones.

lesson 18

Full Armor of God

Aim: Realize that we are doing battle with unseen powers.

Theme: Take both defensive and offensive actions by living the truth, living righteously, bringing forth the gospel of peace and salvation, and living the Word of God — and through prayer and actions!

HOOK ▶ Participants get a cardboard shield and markers, glue, and other art materials as they enter. They are invited to enter the battle of the Lord!

BOOK ▶ Ephesians 6:10-20. Read the Scripture dramatically, or read verses 10-20 and then read the poem "The Sword of the Spirit" (Resource 8). For more effect, make a big wooden sword with "The Word of God" written on it. Other armor also can be made of cardboard.

LOOK ▶ Explanation/Exploration: In a dramatic way, go over the symbolism of each piece of armor. Give some examples of each one, for example: *The helmet of truth means that your life is truthful and your actions match your words.* Tell a story about each one. Another option is to have small groups discuss and come up with a skit or other way to express the meaning for each of the armor pieces. Then they present their ideas or skit for the larger group.

Activity: Direct participants to decorate their shields with each of these ideas: living truth, gospel of peace, salvation, living word, prayer, or any other aspect they want to remember.

TOOK ▶ Each person presents one or more of the pictures on his or her shield. Participants are encouraged to take their armor home. Hanging it up for a week can remind them of the life we are called to lead — it is a battle!

Center of Interest ▶ Cardboard shields, picture of full armor, pieces of armor, big wooden sword.

lesson 19

Listening to the Spirit of God

Aim: Discover ways to get quiet and listen to the Holy Spirit.

Theme: Here is a simple truth that is often overlooked: We need no one to teach us. This is not to say that we are so smart, but that we can go directly to the Holy Spirit and listen quietly. Even children can do this, perhaps even better than adults with noisy and worried minds.

HOOK ▶ As people enter the room, ask each person individually to remain quiet. You can have soft music playing.

BOOK ▶ 1 John 2:27-28.
Read and reread this to the group.

LOOK ▶ Introduce the idea that we live noisy lives with numerous distractions, but we have a rich store of wisdom and peace right inside our hearts: the Spirit of Christ. Let adults or older ones help the younger ones while you teach relaxing and getting quiet. Provide instructions in handout form and/or write the key words on a flipchart. For kids, draw pictures (for example, *relax* is a face with eyes closed, *release* is a stick person with hands raised and things flying away).

Relax

Get comfortable (sitting or reclining); slowly (counting to ten) let your breath out; hold your breath out (counting to five); breathe in deeply (counting to ten) by filling your abdomen and then your upper chest with air; hold your breath in (counting to five). Counting and breathing slowly are essential. At the end of five to ten breaths, you will feel very relaxed; breathe normally and you are ready for the next step.

Release

Once you are relaxed, there is a tendency to become distracted. Thoughts come into your mind that may cause you to drift away from the task at hand. When that happens, let each thought go by saying softly: "I release this into your hands, God." When all thoughts cease, wait silently.

Reflect

You may wish to read a portion of Scripture or other spiritual reading and just wait silently. As distracting thoughts come in, repeat the Release step above.

Receive

Pray: "Jesus, help me to see what you want me to see." Wait for God's still *small voice* to answer.

Respond

What new bit of wisdom have you added to your life this day? What positive change will you commit to as a result? What action will you take?

Is anyone willing to share what they heard and what they might do with this revelation? Get into small groups or pairs (kids and older ones are one unit) and share whatever you feel comfortable sharing.

TOOK ▶ One more silent time. End in prayer thanking God for the messages and asking God to help us become silent and listen more often.

Center of Interest ▶ Meditative music, chairs are rearranged to set a different mood (facing outward or scattered randomly).

lesson 20
The River of Life

Aim: Realize how the story ends.

Theme: Here is a wonderful picture of how things come out in the end. Jesus asks us to keep the faith because he will certainly be triumphant. God's glorious river is a glimpse of heaven to remember and capture in a drawing.

HOOK ▶ Explain that in the end there will be a battle between Satan and the angels of God's heaven. The battle of "Armageddon" takes one verse: Revelation 20:10!

BOOK ▶ Revelation 22:1-7. Read this dramatically.

LOOK ▶ Explanation/Exploration: Assign small groups the key portions of the Scripture and go over them. Ask adults to help kids remember the description of the river and its surroundings. Next, pass out art materials such as magazines, paper, colored pens, tape, and glue. In small groups or as individuals, participants create a picture of what they imagine heaven will be like. When everyone is finished, display the pictures for all to see, and save them, inviting other people to visit the gallery of God's heaven!

Have a big party to celebrate the victory and wonder of God's heaven.

TOOK ▶ Give everyone a card with this message from Revelation 22:7 (CEV): "Remember, I am coming soon! God will bless everyone who pays attention to the message of this book."

Center of Interest ▶ No need for the center of interest; it is created out of the artwork of the participants.

resource 2

Fourteen Scripture Outlines for Intergenerational Programs

The following are outlines of various portions of Scripture. Using the principles and examples in this book, you can create Intergenerational Programs from them.

Joshua and Jericho

Josh. 1:1-5, 6-9, 10-11, 16-18	Responding to God's Voice
Josh. 2:1-12; Heb. 11:31	Rahab: Who God Uses
Josh. 2:12-21	The Scarlet Cord—Foreshadowing Jesus as Savior
Josh. 3:1-17	How God Works: Crossing the Jordan River at Flood Stage
Josh. 4:1-24	Remembering Our God Who Saves
Josh. 5:13-15; 6:1-20; Heb. 11:30	God's Power

Genesis: 7 Days of Creation

Gen. 1:1-5	Day 1: Light!—The Light of the World
Gen. 1:6-8	Day 2: Night and Day—Creation's Contrasts
Gen. 1:9-13	Day 3: Plants—Fruit Bearing
Gen. 1:14-19	Day 4: Season—The Cycles of Life
Gen. 1:10-23	Day 5: Life-giving Air and Water
Gen. 1:24-30	Day 6: Human and Animal Life—God's Creatures
Gen. 1:31; 2:1-3	Day 7: It Was Very Good!—Made in God's Image

Genesis: God and Humanity

Gen. 2:4-17	The Garden—God's Gift 1
Gen. 2:19-20a	The Animals—God's Gift 2
Gen. 2:18, 20b-25	The Family—God's Gift 3
Gen. 3:1-7	The Snake—Rejecting God's Gifts
Gen. 3:8-13, 21-24	The Tree of Life—God's Ultimate Gift

The Song of Moses

Exod. 15:1-5	The Reminder of the Red Sea Crossing
Exod. 15:5-8	The Wonders of God—The Surging Waters Stood Like a Wall
Exod. 15:9-10	God Fights Our Battles!
Exod. 15:11-16	God Makes Us Victorious!
Exod. 15:17-18	God's Reigns in Our Hearts Forever!

Joseph

Gen. 37:1-11	Dreams of Joseph
Gen. 37:12-28	Revenge in the Field
Gen. 37:29-36	Deception of Jacob
Gen. 39:1-20	Potiphar's House—Blessing, Buffeting, Betrayal
Gen. 39:21-23; 40:1-23	Surviving in Prison

Bible Romances: Relationships

Gen. 2:15–3:24	Adam and Eve—Taking the Fall
Gen. 15:1-6; 16:1-16; 18:1-15; 21:1-8	Abraham and Sarah—Weathering Storms
Gen. 24:1-67	Isaac and Rebecca—True Love, Love True
Gen. 29:1-35; 30:22-23	Jacob and Rachael (and Leah)—Faithfulness
Ruth	Ruth and Boaz—We Need Each Other

Early David

1 Sam. 15:1-23	Saul Rejected
1 Sam. 17:32-37	Lions and Bears
1 Sam. 16:1-13	Chosen and Anointed
1 Sam. 16:14-23	The King's Musician
1 Sam. 17:1-11, 26-54	Giant Killing
Heb. 12:1-2; John 8:31-36	Conquering Giants: How It's Done!

Ruth: Friendship

Ruth 1:1-5	Friends Face Trouble
Ruth 1:6-22	Friends Make Difficult Decisions
Ruth 2:1-23	Making New Friends Means Working
Ruth 3:1-18	Friendship Deepens
Ruth 4:1-21	Friendship Rewarded

The Flood and Faithfulness

Gen. 5:32; 6:5-13	Foul Players and Faithful Followers (Faith = Holiness)
Gen. 6:14—7:16	Fixing and Filling the Ark (Faith = Obedience)
Gen. 7:17—8:12	Flooding and Floating (Faith = Trusting)
Gen. 8:13-22	Finally Landing (Faith = Worship)
Gen. 9:1-17	Forever Covenant (Faith = Hopefulness)

Jonah

Jonah 1:14-16	Sea Voyage—A Splashing Drama
Jonah 1:17—2:9	Whale of a Time—In the Belly
Jonah 2:10—3:3	Being Released—Saying Yes to God's Call
Jonah 3:4-10	Nineveh—Time to Preach Repentance
Jonah 4:1-10	Vine, Worm, and Wind
Luke 11:29-32	The Sign of Jonah—Celebration of Jesus' Victory!

God's Water Works and Wonders

Gen. 1:6-10, 20-23	Story of Water—Life
Gen. 6—9	The Flood Story—Grace
Ex. 14	The Parting of the Red Sea—Help
Luke 8:22-25	Jesus Calms the Storm—Faith
John 21:1-14	Fish for Breakfast—Sharing

Living Simply in a Complex World

Eccl. 2:24-26; 3:1-8	This American Life—Chasing after Wind?
Matt. 5:1-10	Power Down—Finding True Life
Matt. 6:19-21; Psalm 39:11	Treasures on Earth or in Heaven?
Psalm 24:1; 36:6-7; 104	Caring about God's Creation
Gen. 2:15	Getting It Right—My Decision

The Life of Christ

Luke 2:8-14	Birth—God Gives His Only Child
Matt. 3:11-17	Baptism of Jesus—Dedication of Our Lives
Luke 6:27-36	Ministry—Teaching Love
John 19:16-18, 28-30	Crucifixion—Perfect Love, Rejected
Luke 24:1-12	Resurrection—Victory, Power, Redemption, and Life!

The First Titanic: Paul's Shipwreck

Acts 23:11; 26:32; 27:1-12	The Journey—God's Plan for Our Lives
Acts 27:13-26	The Storm—Facing God's Challenges
Acts 27:27-44	The Shipwreck—God's Providence
Acts 28:1-6	The Bonfire—God's Protection
Acts 28:7-10	The Healing—God Heals

resource 3

Poetry as Prayer Intergenerational Program

A small group of children and adults gather in the classroom. The group consists of a couple of preschool kids, three elementary-age kids, two young teenagers, and seven adults. The leader, Robin, begins by having the group sing the song "As the Deer" (Psalm 42). Next she hands out a sheet of paper with a matrix. Across the top are listed three kinds of prayers: praise, petition, and pronouncement. Along the side are listed three kinds of poems: list (a poem made up of a list), lune (a simple three-line poem), and a "let it fly" poem (any form you like). So there are nine sample poem-prayers in the nine spaces of the matrix, mainly taken from Psalms, and a couple that Robin made up.

"I want to introduce you to one type of prayer and several types of poems this week," Robin begins to explain. Then she reads the samples of praise poems. She even makes up a couple on the spot and writes them on the whiteboard.

"Next, I want you to gather into groups of four or five with at least two kids or a youth, and two adults in each group." They form groups.

"Now take a couple of minutes to come up with what the word *praise* means." The groups do this. And Robin asks each group to share its definition.

"Now I want everyone to write a praise poem. We'll learn the other types of poems in our next classes. You adults help the younger ones with ideas and write for them if they can't write. You have ten minutes for this. Perfection is not the goal—just let words flow."

The groups get busy right away and Robin goes from group to group helping the little ones and adults as well.

After ten minutes, Robin says, "Now read your poems to each other, and then when you are ready we'll hear everyone's poems. Big people will read for the little ones."

The group hears lovely recitations of each praise poem and applauds each. Robin collects the poems and announces plans to have them printed for everyone to enjoy. The group goes out, talking about praise poems and everyone seems to be inspired.

In both adult education and in education in general, active learning is very important. Teachers must engage the whole person, using a variety of methods, to increase learning. Greater learning results from greater involvement of the learner; learners must be hearing, seeing, saying, and doing something with the Scripture. Greater involvement = greater learning (See Figure 3.3 in Chapter Three).

As I mentioned earlier, if you take this one step further and have participants teaching each other, there is greater learning still. This is why small groups working together to present ideas to other groups become so vital in IP as we grapple with Bible truths (I cover the use of small groups in Chapter Seven: Design and Develop). I also introduced the idea of learning modes in Chapter Six: Lesson-Planning Process. Using either learning mode helps you make Scripture learning active. It involves the use of these two learning modes:

Explanation/Exploration

and its inverse......

Exploration/Explanation

There are two aspects of the learning modes.

(1) *Explanation:* The leader teaches, demonstrates, and illustrates the key principles or knowledge that participants need. Or the leader may draw from discoveries the participants make in exploring the Bible truths. The leader gathers information, helps participants analyze and think through various ideas. When participants hear or read lessons or when they recount or report the various things learned, this is explanation. In this aspect the learners listen, read, take notes, absorb facts, think, and analyze.

(2) *Exploration:* The teacher or participants create experiences that engage the learners through seeing, discussing, doing, and teaching each other. The learners practice, experiment, try out, take risks, and discover new learning. These can include any activities related to the topic of study.

Deconstructing Poetry and Prayer

Robin was using the *Explanation* aspect when she explained about types of prayer and poetry. When she asked the groups to write praise poems and share them she was using the *Exploration* aspect. When she asked the groups to come up with what they thought praise was, she was having the participants *teach* each other. Her learning mode was Explanation/Exploration. She first taught the group and let participants discover the meaning of praise (Explanation), and then she directed them to create their own praise poems and share them with their small groups and then with the whole group (Exploration).

> In another week's lesson, Robin begins with another song: "The Name of the Lord" (is a strong and mighty tower...). She directs people into small groups again, and gives each group a sheet of flipchart paper and a pen.
>
> "This week we will be looking at pronouncement prayers—prayers that tell about the wonders and works of God. I want you to list some of the things you like about God and some of the things that God does for you or for the world. Make up as many as you can." The groups get busy listing and writing these things. As Robin makes her rounds to the groups, she hears some examples by the preschoolers that confirm for her they are on the right track: "God helped my daddy get a job." "God loves me this I know." The adults write these on the sheets.
>
> Robin breaks in after a few minutes: "Now make up a pronouncement poem as a group. A list poem would work just great with these things you named." The groups get involved in creating a group poem. Then each group reads their poems, to applause. A few tears are shed by a couple of older folks when they hear such wonderful things about God's love and care.
>
> After the readings, Robin asks the group what they think pronouncement prayers are.
>
> "Listing good stuff about God," answers Tony, an elementary student.
>
> "Saying what things God does for us," Mr. Winthrop speaks up.

The group lists many ideas and Robin sums up the contributions. She then uses the song "The Name of the Lord" as an example of a pronouncement, even saying what the righteous should do: "Run into the name of the Lord!"

Robin offers to have the pronouncement poems added to their "poetry as prayer" booklet.

This time Robin used the other mode for the lesson: Exploration/Explanation. She got the group singing, coming up with ideas, writing, and then reading their contributions. She followed this up with more explanation of what a pronouncement prayer is and gave examples of it. She even tied it into the song they learned from Scripture.

GOING INTERGENERATIONAL

	PRAISE & THANKS	**PETITION**	**PRONOUNCEMENT**

LIST POEM — Add a list of items to your poem	**Psalm 148:1-4**
	
	Praise the Lord from the heavens!
	Praise him from the skies!
	Praise him, all his angels!
	Praise him, all the armies of heaven!
	Praise him, sun and moon!
	Praise him, all you twinkling stars!
	Praise him, skies above!
	Praise him, vapors
	   high above the clouds!
		Beach Prayer
		
		Oh setter of the sun
		Oh maker of the sea
		Oh mover of the tide
		Comfort me
		Oh bringer of the rain
		Oh grower of seaweed
		Oh churner of the waves
		Meet my need
		
		(Jim Teeters)
			Let nothing disturb you,
			Nothing frighten you;
			All things are passing;
			God never changes;
			Patient endurance
			   attains all things
			Who God possesses
			   in nothing is wanting;
			Alone God suffices.
			
			(Teresa of Avila–written on a bookmark found in her Breviary)

LUNE — first line 3 words, second line 5 words, third line 3 words	Thank you God For hills, flowers; a tree Thanks for me! My hands raised My head bowed, saying thanks I laugh aloud! *(Jim Teeters)*	Give us peace Let your boat of love Sail through me. Let my heart break like glass for my brother in war. *(Jim Teeters)*	My soul thirsts For the wine and milk of your grace All the world longs like hungry birds for your salvation, Lord! *(Jim Teeters)*

LET IT FLY — anything-style poem–freestyle	**I gazed at God and laughed**
	
	amazed
	I thought He'd frown at me and chide
	but no, instead his smile was wide
	
	I gazed at God and laughed
	   surprised
	by the love, the mercy the grace
	the smile on my redeemer's face
	
	I gazed at God and laughed
	   relieved
	I laid down all my fears and raced
	headlong to God and we embraced
	
	A joyous sound was heard that day
	the curtain tore and split apart
	I felt God's spirit change my heart
	
	(Jim Teeters)
		Lean Way into Life (A Prayer)
		
		Thank you for my life, varied
		   mysterious
		      creative
		         mundane
		wild and ordinary
		
		Let
		me not get caught in dry duty
		   just live the wonder
		      of it all
		         heartfelt
		send me forth with laughter
		
		May
		my life be filled with wisdom
		   and humility
		      satisfied
		         yet empty
		
		Help me
		lean way into life
		   as over a cliff
		with faith
		
		(Jim Teeters)
			Psalm 42:1-3
			
			A white-tailed deer drinks from the creek;
			I want to drink God, deep draughts of God.
			I'm thirsty for God-alive.
			I wonder, "Will I ever make it–arrive and drink in God's presence?"
			I'm on a diet of tears–
			   tears for breakfast,
			   tears for supper.
			All day long
			   People knock at my door,
			Pestering,
			   "Where is this God of yours?"
			
			(The Message)
			
			A fish cannot drown in water
			A bird does not fall in air
			In the fire of its making,
			Gold doesn't vanish:
			The fire brightens.
			Each creature God made
			Must live in its own nature;
			How could I resist my nature
			That lives for oneness with God?
			
			(Mechtild of Magdeburg)

resource 4

Intergenerational Programming in a Family Camp

Making the transition from traditional family camping (keynote speaker, separate classes for kids and adults) to Intergenerational Programming (IP) will take some planning and public-relations efforts. Further efforts will need to be made when you involve participants in program design and operations, because the usual pattern is for people to show up at the camp setting and find that the program is planned for them. But in participant-integrated programming (PIP), groups of participants are responsible for helping design and put on certain portions of the program. This can be quite a shift from leader-planned camps that folks have become used to—shifting from *"we go to camp and things happen"* to *"we go to camp and create the program ourselves."*

Leader-Planned Family Camp

In a leader-planned family camp the whole camp is designed and set up by the leadership, and participants come and enjoy the experience of IP. This is less risky than PIP camps where programs are planned by participants. The planning begins with a group or committee, and the following staffing functions must be covered:

Direction – Responsibility for facility negotiations; recruiting, staffing, and supervision; financial planning and budgeting; and general administration.

Publicity – Getting the word out in an attractive way.

Safety and medical – First aid, water safety, sanitation, etc.

Program – Creating the theme and scriptural lessons, as well as planning and recruiting staff or volunteers in any or all aspects of the program, including guest speaker, arts-and-crafts facilitator, special outings coordinator, music director, food-service staff.

Guest speaker – Provides short, inspirational teachings based on event themes geared for *all* ages.

Materials, supplies, and equipment

Arts and crafts

Music – Planning song services, theme songs, wake-up song surprises.

Food service – Providing regular meals and snacks, special theme food, and sanitation.

Special features of the camp setting – Coordinating boating, hiking, sight-seeing, sports options, etc. These activities are available during the free (unscheduled) times.

Evaluation and follow-up

Typical Daily Schedule for Family Camp

7:30 a.m. Wake up songs — Singers, accompanied by guitar or flute, wander through the camp like morning minstrels singing a theme song as a welcome to the morning and the day's activities. This feature brings sleepy smiles, laughter, and sets a joyful tone that kids love. The song also starts the teaching — as the minstrels wander, other campers join the fun.

8:30 a.m. Breakfast — The day's schedule is posted and announcements are made.

10:00 a.m. Event and lesson in the chapel — This starts with singing fun and inspirational songs and leads into the theme song and the day's lesson. The lesson and learning activities are followed by a short talk by the guest speaker.

11:00 a.m. Free time

12:00 noon Boxed lunch

12:30 p.m. Free time and activities

5:30 p.m. Dinner (special BBQ and theme food)

7:00 p.m. Event and lesson at the campfire circle — This starts with singing fun and inspirational songs and leads into the theme song and the evening's lesson. The lesson and learning activities take place with a brief follow-up talk by the guest speaker.

8:30 p.m. Talent show and snacks (or similar after-hours event)

9:30 p.m. Bedtime

10:00 p.m. All quiet!

Participant-Integrated Programming (PIP)

Remember this principle of learning: Those who teach learn best! That is the principle behind PIP, in which the participants take a large role in the teaching of others. A smaller camp (fifty to eighty) is simpler to design for PIP. When a family-and-friends camp is larger (one hundred to two hundred), PIP gets more complex but is still possible with a strong organization and with more staff or volunteer leaders. If a camp is designed with five or six events, the staff leadership designs and puts on the first event as a model for others. Then the camp is divided into teams who plan the other events with the help of a guide sheet as well as any staff who act as consultants. You can also train volunteer facilitators to help the teams put on the events. I have been amazed and inspired over and over to watch a team of adults, youth, and kids put together an event. A Sample Planning Guide Sheet is shown at the end of this section.

Participant Involvement Plan (PIP):
A Participant Group Plans an Event

"Okay, listen up! Here is our assignment." The leader, Lucy, reads from the Guide Sheet and announces that they have been assigned the story of the Israelites grumbling and then God providing them manna. "First we have to read over the story a couple of times. Mark, you and Amy take your group and do that. I'll stay here with the rest of us."

Each group has eight participants with preschoolers through adults. They spend a few minutes reading over Exodus 16:1-4, 13-19, with emphasis on the manna. Mark and Lucy make sure the kids understand the story.

"Okay, let's decide in our separate groups the most important lesson in this story." Lucy returns to her group, and Mark and Amy get their group discussing. After a few minutes Lucy gets everyone together.

"What do you think is the key point here?" Amy points to Kimberly, a bright-eyed eleven-year-old who says, "We talked about the Lord's Prayer and how this is like trusting God to give you your daily bread. We must trust God."

"Daily," George chimes in. Everyone nods.

"Okay, let's make that our lesson. Trusting God! But how are we going to show what trust is?"

"I know an exercise in trust!" Karen is a social worker and is used to this kind of stuff. "We have people in groups of eight or so. A person stands in the center and the rest make a circle around him or her. The person in the center is blindfolded and keeps his or her feet together and then leans back. The group members put out their arms and slowly, gently pass that person around the circle."

"What about kids?" adds Tom, "Can they keep an adult up?"

"You pair a kid with an adult who does most of the pushing. I've seen this done and it really gets you in touch with trust—kids, too."

"Another idea is the trust walk," adds Timmy, a high school youth. "Each person takes a turn with a partner and then they are led around blindfolded."

"I got it!" Lucy's eyes are wide with discovery. "How about we divide the campers into teams of eight or nine with parents watching out for kids, and then the group can choose which they want to try—trust walk or falling back and getting moved around."

This gets everyone excited. This is what they want to do. Later the details are worked out and these are the group's notes:

Title: In God We Trust—Daily!

Song to start: "'Tis So Sweet to Trust in Jesus"

Talk 1: Cameron will review briefly the story of Exodus, including our part in it.

Activity: Groups of eight to ten will choose "Trust Walk" or "Fall Back and Get Moved Around"—people play with these two activities. Ask groups to talk about trust as they do this. Answer the question: What is trust?

Talk 2: Lucy will ask: "What does this teach us about trusting God daily?" She'll put the ideas on a flipchart. Our group will give a big cheer for each idea to reward the offering.

Song to end: "Trust and Obey"

Prayer: Prayer for greater trust and then pray "The Lord's Prayer."

If people are given an opportunity and a little help to be creative program planners, they will come forth with some great teaching. Part of the pressure for the participant is to succeed. I have never found a PIP group to risk not doing the best job they can. One final point: You need to give an opportunity for people to get involved or to step out if they feel uncomfortable. Let the groups know that they must not try to force anyone—adult or child—into something that makes that person feel uncomfortable.

Good Planning!

Whether you decide to conduct leader-planned camp or use the PIP approach is up to the overall planning group who know their people and what works best. I encourage you to step out and go for greater participant involvement, but do what seems best for your church or organization. There are plenty of ideas for a curriculum in Resources 1 and 2. The leader and planning groups can change or add to the designs as needed. Good planning!

Sample Planning Guide Sheet

Instructions:

Your small group will be planning an activity to help the whole group learn from the Scripture. Here is a list of steps to help you:

1. Meet together and select a leader. The leader's job will be to guide the group planning process and see that everyone has an opportunity to participate, including the youngest child who is able. The leader should be someone able and willing.

2. Read over your assigned Scripture as a group or have one person read it. Then read it again.

3. List the most important ideas in the Scripture passage. Then as a group decide on the one most important thing you will want the participants to learn. What main idea would be most helpful to them?

4. Plan an event based on your assigned Scripture.
    a. Remember you have to keep within your scheduled time.
    b. Here is how to structure your event:
     1. Do a brief recap of the previous event and the story or Scripture lesson. Give us a brief outline of your portion of the Scripture. (3-5 minutes)
     2. Plan an activity that will help us learn that one most important idea. It is important to involve everyone and we must be doing something to help us learn. (30 minutes)
     3. Take us "deeper" with a special teaching or enlist the participants' help in identifying the most important ideas. (5-7 minutes)

5. Helpful Hints
    a. The church staff is available for consultation and assistance.
    b. If you need special props, go searching or ask a leader; we have materials available for you.
    c. Consider the whole facility available for your activity.
    d. You may ask any willing participant to help you with your activity.
    e. Suggest songs to the music team (to begin and to end the activity).

Choose from any of these ideas for an activity:

- Games • Drama • Challenges • Costumes
- Arts and Crafts • Prizes • Movement or Dance
- Music • Adventures • Skits • Natural Environment
- Radio Theater • Constructions • Board Games
- Races and Relays • Other Scriptures • Simulations

resource 5

'Alice the Camel' Game

"Alice the Camel" Lyrics

Writer Unknown

Alice the camel has five humps.
Alice the camel has five humps.
Alice the camel has five humps.
So go, Alice, go.

Alice the camel has four humps.
Alice the camel has four humps.
Alice the camel has four humps.
So go, Alice, go.

Alice the camel has three humps.
Alice the camel has three humps.
Alice the camel has three humps.
So go, Alice, go.

Alice the camel has two humps.
Alice the camel has two humps.
Alice the camel has two humps.
So go, Alice, go.

Alice the camel has one hump.
Alice the camel has one hump.
Alice the camel has one hump.
So go, Alice, go.

Alice the camel has no humps.
Alice the camel has no humps.
Alice the camel has no humps.
Because Alice is a horse!

Instructions

1. Everyone forms a circle and holds hands.
2. As people start singing they start walking around clockwise with small steps.
3. When they sing *go*, the group takes three tiny jumps toward the center and all yell: BOOM, BOOM, BOOM (it is nonsense, but fun).
4. On to the next stanza and circling again.

As the group gets to the end of the song, the circle becomes more and more compact, until the last stanza, when the leader yells "Because Alice is a horse!" By then there is a "crush" of people and it is time to enjoy the closeness. Encourage hugs and if it is the end of the time together, people can say their goodbyes amid the laughter.

For an approximate tune check out:
http://www.youtube.com/watch?v=UmR_PCEgd4I

resource 6

Elevator to Judgment Drama

Scripture basis: Luke 18:9-14; Gal. 3:10, 11; Eph. 2:8, 9

Cast:
  St. Peter
  Jesus
  3-5 Self-Righteous people (SR)
  2-3 Sinners

Scene 1: The foyer of the Elevator to Judgment

(Both *Sinners* and *Self-Righteous* are gathering near the elevator. *Righteous* are looking confident, *Sinners* looking nervous.)

Self-Righteous 1 (SR-1): (to no one in particular) All of a sudden a no-good, stinking driver hits me while I was innocently walking home from Bible study. Now I'm here—what is this place?

SR- 2: I guess we are headed for judgment. I got a high fever—next thing I know I'm here. See it says, "Elevator to Judgment." But I got no worry; I've been pretty good; gave my tithe, taught Sunday school.

SR-2: Same here, I'm morally fit as a fiddle.

SR-3: Well, I was simply hang-gliding—a big updraft—and here I am facing the judgment. Lucky for us we are pure as the driven wind! (Laughs.)

(All SRs laugh)

Sinner-1: (to no one in particular) Boy, I was down on my luck, left my wife, no luck. I got some bad dope, and now...look at me. Dead!

Sinner-2: Well, I was headed out of the bank with 100 Gs I robbed, the cops met me, and next thing I know...I am scared, I don't mind tellin' ya. I ain't no saint.

Sinner-1: (Nods knowingly) Yeah, me too...I sure have made a mess of my life.

SR-1 and SR-2: (Shoves S-1 and S-2 away and all together say) Well, get away from us!

SR-2: We don't need to have you sliming up our lives, scum!

St. Peter: (Appears as elevator doors open) Okay, everyone, listen up. Get in the Elevator to Judgment; all the righteous on my right and all sinners on my left—hurry now.

Scene 2: Elevator

(The Self-Righteous quickly line up and stand upright, looking snooty, and self-righteous, while the Sinners cower on St. Peter's left.)

St. Peter: (Pushes button) All right, here we go. You will see *Jesus* at last!

Sinners: (All together) Oh dear!

(Everyone in elevator slowly turn around to the left to indicate the elevator is ascending.)

St. Peter: (Pushes the button) Heaven!

Jesus: (Jesus appears) Welcome to my heaven.

Sinners: (Drop to their knees; all together say) Lord have mercy on us *Sinners!*

Jesus: All on Peter's left please step on in to heaven—your sins are forgiven.

Self-Righteous: (Look stunned, gasp, "What?" etc.)

St. Peter: Going down!

(Everyone in elevator slowly turn around to the right to indicate the elevator is descending.)

St. Peter: (Pushes the button) All righteous on my right, all *Sinners* to my left!

Self-Righteous: (All the SRs rush to the left of *St. Peter*)

St. Peter: (Pushes the button)

(Everyone in elevator slowly turn around to the left to indicate the elevator is ascending.)

St. Peter: (Pushes the button) Heaven!

Jesus: (Jesus appears) Welcome to my heaven.

Self-Righteous: (Drop to their knees; all together) Lord have mercy on us *Sinners!*

Jesus: All on Peter's left please step on in to heaven—your sins are forgiven.

Everyone lines up, faces the audience, and bows.

resource 7

Parable of the Sower—Combined Scripture

Matthew 13:1-9, 18-23

[1] That same day Jesus went out of the house and sat by the lake.

[2] Such large crowds gathered around him that he got into a boat and sat in it, while all the people stood on the shore.

[3] Then he told them many things in parables, saying: A farmer went out to sow his seed.

[4] As he was scattering the seed, some fell along the path, and the birds came and ate them up. Listen then to what the parable means:

[19] When anyone hears the message about the kingdom and does not understand it, the evil one comes and snatches away what was sown in his heart. This is the seed sown along the path.

[5] Some fell on rocky places, where it did not have much soil. It sprang up quickly, because the soil was shallow.

[6] But when the sun came up, the plants were scorched, and they withered because they had no root. Listen then to what the parable means:

[20] The one who received the seed that fell on rocky places is the one who hears the word and at once receives it with joy.

[21] But since he has no root, he lasts only a short time. When trouble or persecution comes because of the word, he quickly falls away.

[7] Other seed fell among thorns, which grew up and choked the plants. Listen then to what the parable means:

[22] The one who received the seed that fell among the thorns is the one who hears the word, but the worries of this life and the deceitfulness of wealth choke it, making it unfruitful.

[8] Still other seed fell on good soil, where it produced a crop—a hundred, sixty or thirty times what was sown. Listen then to what the parable means: The one who received the seed that fell on good soil is the one who hears the word and understands it. He produces a crop, yielding a hundred, sixty or thirty times what was sown.

[9] He who has ears, let him hear.

resource 8

Poem: The Sword of the Spirit
the Word of God*

Hold the sword, feel its balance
Swing it around awhile to
Get the feel of it
Thaw-whack it into a tree
Get the sense of its power
"Bring the devil on!" you say
"Fight to the finish," you say

Ah, now that you have God's mighty Spirit in your hands
Will you really wield it? Can you face the enemy?
Do you feel invincible?

Better slip on the belt of truth
The only thing that is strong enough to hold
Such a sword
Place the breastplate of righteousness over your frail rib cage to
Protect your heart
Wear shoes that are ready to make peace, in case the sword is too hard to handle
Carry the shield of faith because sometimes the enemy
Strikes from afar with flaming arrows
Designed to weaken you, make you afraid
And the helmet of salvation—put it on
It lets the devil know you mean business

Now remember once you're dressed that way
You are pretty easy to spot
Your armor gleams and you move slowly
The sword of God can get very heavy
Best drop to your knees and pray
For yourself, for others, pray for me
Kneel reverently as the beads of sweat
Make their way down your cheeks
And drip like cold needles along your neck
Okay, get on your feet.
Are you READY?

*Ephesians 6:10-20

resource 9

Warm-up Activities for All Ages

Introduction

Before listing and describing these special activities, let's look at the reasons for using them in Intergenerational Programming. You use them:

1. To aid **transition** from everyday life to the learning situation.

2. To aid in **relaxation** so people feel more free and open to take part.

3. To aid in the **connection** between people who may not know each other very well.

4. To aid **concentration** by helping participants focus attention on the task at hand.

5. To aid **motivation** by helping participants feel at ease and ready to learn.

6. To aid **communication** by helping participants learn cooperatively.

With small children, it is best to for kids to join with a parent or older child. Often the actions and laughter spill over and all ages enjoy an activity even if they are not fully aware of its meaning.

Activities

1. Tell about Your Favorite...

Purpose: Get to know each other and/or summarize a topic.
Procedure: 1. Groups of two to six
2. People share their favorite Scripture, Bible character, animal, etc. in their small group.
3. Next people tell what makes it their favorite.
4. When sharing is over, volunteers can share their favorites with the larger group.
Option: After the lesson, people can share their favorite thing about the lesson or favorite thing they learned.

2. U R Unique

Purpose: Have some fun sharing talents and learn about each other in new ways.

Procedure: 1. Group size can vary.

2. What little-known talent do you have, or what unusual thing can you do? Are you double-jointed? Can you cross your eyes or walk on your hands? Let each person think about that for awhile and then let everyone show their unique skill to others. Have fun learning.

Variation: Reveal something about yourself that no one knows about you.

3. We Are All the Same

Purpose: Explore similarities in each other. It is just plain fun.

Procedure: 1. Groups of three to seven.

2. The activity begins by listing things group members may have in common. Ignore the obvious (two eyes, hair on our head) and go for the oddities (we all love cats, like crunchy cereal, have a fear of spiders). Try to discover the weirdest or funniest commonality. When done, groups can share their discoveries with the larger group.

Variation: Go on to list things that make each person different from one another — what none of them has in common.

4. Top of My Head

Purpose: To share what is on your mind.

Procedure: 1. Group size can vary.

2. Pick a partner and say the first thing that comes into your mind, and repeat as often as people stay interested. Change partners, or join to form a group of four.

Variation: Try to explain why that idea popped into your head.

5. Group Aeronautical Designers

Purpose: Group building, teaching about acceptance, having some fun.

Procedure:
1. Groups of two to six.
2. Give each group a single piece of paper (of any variety or size).
3. Group members should design and fold their paper into a dynamic, accurate, and long-range airplane in reparation for a contest. No fair testing it before the contest.
4. Each group takes turns tossing their creation toward a target at some distance away.
5. Important: No matter how well the airplane flies, instruct the group to clap and cheer loudly for each team!
6. The winner, as well as the others, gets a prize.

Variation:
a. Instruct teams to test and modify their plane before the contest.
b. Share a little devotional thought on how the cheering is similar to how God sees us, in Christ, and cheers for us regardless of how well we perform.

6. Huddle (or Hug)

Purpose: Just plain fun and warms people up.

Procedure:
1. Large groups.
2. The leader instructs people to mill around in the room or designated area.
3. The leader calls out "huddle" or "hug" and then names a characteristic like shirt color, type of shoes, or hair length and people with similar characteristics quickly huddle together or hug.

Variation:
a. Call out favorites (like same animal, same color, or same beverage) and people have to figure out how to find their group.
b. Limit the size of the huddle or hug group.
c. Use this method to form groups for the next activity.

7. I Want to Know

Purpose: Participants decide what they want to know about others and then go find out.

Procedure:
1. Group size can vary.
2. Start by asking participants to think of something that would be fun or interesting to know about other people.
3. Ask participants to think of a question to ask.
4. Instruct participants to mill around and when you give a signal, they should stop and face the nearest person and exchange questions and answers. Repeat this for as long as folks seem interested.

Variation:
a. Change questions and repeat.
b. Ask people to think up actions they want performed (for example, say a poem, tell a joke, do a dance). Watch out; this can get wild!

8. Milling

Purpose: Have fun and get acquainted.

Procedure:
1. Large groups.
2. Instruct all participants to mill around.
3. When you give the signal, participants meet in groups of three.
4. The leader has questions ready and the groups share their answers. Some possibilities: What would you wish for if you had three wishes? What would you do with a million dollars? What did you think of a (specific) parable? Relate the questions to the theme or aim of the lesson.
5. Keep this up with new topics as long as people seem happy and interested.

9. A Rain Storm Comes and Goes

Purpose: Relax and prepare for prayer or silent contemplation.

Procedure:
1. Groups of ten or more.
2. Instruct the group to form a circle.
3. Ask everyone turn to the right and place their hands on the shoulders of the person in front of them (small kids can place their hands on a person's lower back).
4. The leader pats the shoulders of the person in front of him or her, and the motion passes along until all participants start to do the same. The leader should announce that this is the sound of a storm coming and going. The leader starts harder pats and slowly makes them harder and louder — the "rain" sound gets louder. The leader then reverses the process until the rain sound slowly comes to an end. The leader says: "The storm has come and gone."
5. At this point in the silence the leader instructs the group to pray silently.

10. Re-energizers

Purpose: To energize the group and for just plain fun.

1. Declare a "Rock, Paper, Scissors" tournament.
2. Sing a song in a round — two, three, or four parts.
3. Play "Simon Says" and let various volunteers lead.
4. Play "Follow the Leader" with clapping rhythms. Volunteers take turns leading the clapping patterns, and others repeat those patterns.